THE BIG BOOK OF TRIVIA FUN!

kidsbooks

Visit us at **www.kidsbooks.com**®

INTRODUCTION

Did you know that the original name for ice hockey was hurley? Have you any idea what an otolaryngologist does? What do you suppose is the average life span of a one-dollar bill?

Those and many, many other fascinating trivia tidbits are packed into these pages. As you explore this info-packed megabook, you will learn a zillion cool facts about lots of subjects, including animals, nature, famous people, geography, entertainment, history, sports, the U.S. and its presidents, the human body, science and technology, and language. Amaze and amuse your friends!

There are lots of ways you can put *The Big Book of Trivia Fun* to good use—including having fun!

Ready to go? Turn the page!

CAVE
CANEM

ANIMAL ANTICS

The pattern of stripes on a tiger's face is as unique as a person's fingerprints. No two tigers have the same pattern.

Pigs wallow in mud to cool off because they do not sweat. Also, mud protects their tender skin from sunburn.

The horned toad, a type of lizard, may squirt blood from the corners of its eyes when frightened, though it is more likely to gulp in air to make its body look larger.

A cricket's sense of hearing is located in its legs.

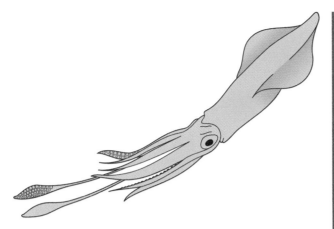

The world's largest invertebrate (an animal without a backbone) is the giant squid, which can be as long as 59 feet.

Sharkskin is 100 times stronger than cowhide.

The Bactrian camel is the only land mammal that can survive by drinking salt water.

Worldwide, there are about 200 separate breeds of purebred dogs.

During its long winter sleep, a black bear can lose 30 to 40 percent of its body weight.

SPORTS STUFF

A served tennis ball can travel almost 150 miles per hour. (Andy Roddick and Greg Rusedski have hit serves clocked at 149 mph!)

Cal Hubbard is the only athlete elected to both the National Baseball Hall of Fame and the professional and collegiate football halls of fame.

In major-league baseball, if a fielder catches a fly ball with his hat instead of his glove, the batter takes two bases.

Janet Guthrie was the first woman to compete in a NASCAR Winston Cup race (1976), the Daytona 500 (1977), and the Indianapolis 500 (1977).

The average NBA basketball lasts for about 10,000 bounces.

The first hockey goalie to wear a mask during games was Jacques Plante of the Montreal Canadiens, in 1959.

The American League was organized in Philadelphia, Pennsylvania, in 1900. It consisted of eight baseball teams. The first AL games were played in 1901.

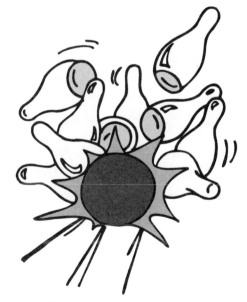

In bowling, three strikes in a row is called a turkey.

The 12 rules of modern boxing, written in 1867, are called the Queensbury rules. They were named after the Marquis of Queensbury, an English nobleman.

Science Fair

On January 1, 1954, NBC aired the first nationwide TV broadcast in color—the Tournament of Roses parade. Most people saw it in black and white, though. The only sets able to display color were 200 tester TVs at various stations around the country.

The first-ever Nobel Prize for Physics was awarded, in 1901, to Wilhelm Konrad Roentgen. In 1895, Roentgen discovered X rays and how they could be used to "see" inside the body. Roentgen's work took modern medicine a giant step forward.

A scientist who specializes in the study of cells is called a *cytologist*.

In 1948, An Wang invented a device known as the magnetic core memory. Wang's device allowed a computer or calculator to hold information in its "memory." It was later set aside by the invention of the microchip, which can hold much more information in a much smaller area.

The skin of an electric eel packs a zap of up to 650 volts—enough power to kill a small animal, and give a human a nasty jolt. This shocking creature can grow to a length of nine feet—about four-fifths of which is its tail.

The first person to make a super-sonic flight—faster than the speed of sound—was Chuck Yeager. On October 14, 1947, at about 40,000 feet above California's Rogers Dry Lake, Yeager piloted an experimental Bell X-1 jet to Mach 1.06—about 700 miles per hour.

If you read movie credits, you have seen Jack Foley's name—or part of it. In the 1930s, Foley was a pioneer in editing sound effects for movies. Today, the *foley* or *Foley artist* is the person who creates and records a movie's sound effects, and matches those sound effects with the action on the screen.

THIS and THAT

Q. Can you write 1776—the year in which the Declaration of Independence was signed—in Roman numerals?

A. MDCCLXXVI (M = 1,000, DCC = 700, LXX = 70, VI = 6)

Q. Can you name all eight of Santa's reindeer from the famous poem written by Clement Clarke Moore in 1922?

A. Dasher, Dancer, Prancer, Vixen, Comet, Cupid, Donder, and Blitzen. (Rudolph the red-nosed reindeer is from a 1939 poem that later became a popular Christmas song.)

Q. The terms *elliptical, irregular, lenticular,* and *spiral* are used to describe different types of what?

A. galaxies

Q. The igloo, a temporary dwelling used by Inuits of northern Canada and Greenland during the winter hunting season, is made of blocks cut from what?

A. snow (not ice)

Q. How did Hercules, hero of Greek myths, purify himself after committing a crime?

A. He performed 12 "impossible" feats, known as the Twelve Labors of Hercules.

Q. New York City's famous Empire State Building has how many windows?

A. 6,500

Q. Which of these is *not* a one-person card game: canfield, klondike, patience, or whist?

A. whist

Q. Do Mexican jumping beans really jump?

A. Yes. Each one has a live, one-quarter inch caterpillar inside. When the caterpillar moves, the bean "jumps."

Q. About how many stone blocks were used to build Egypt's Great Pyramid?

A. 2.3 million

The Amazing U.S.A.

Freedom's Journal, published from 1827 to 1829, was the first newspaper owned and operated by and for African-Americans.

Daylight saving time was first used in the U.S. in 1918, to conserve fuel during World War I.

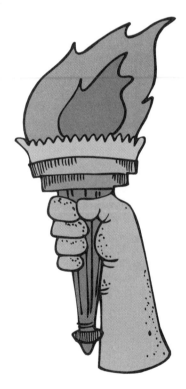

The Statue of Liberty's torch is 29 feet tall, from the tip of the flame to the bottom of the handle.

The Fair Labor Standards Act (also called the Wages and Hours Act) was signed into law on June 14, 1938. It was the first law to limit the number of hours that children could work. It also was the first to protect children from dangerous work.

In 1956, the U.S. Army retired its last unit of pack mules after 125 years of service. The Army had used the mules to haul food, ammunition, and other supplies in hard-to-reach battle areas.

The White House has 132 rooms and 35 bathrooms on six levels.

U.S. paper money was first printed in 1862.

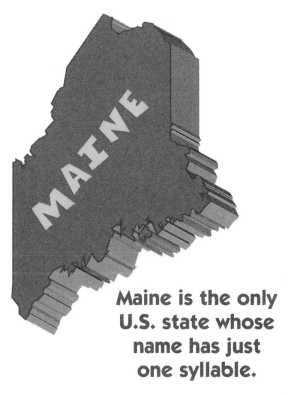

Maine is the only U.S. state whose name has just one syllable.

The first known train robbery in the U.S. took place on October 6, 1866. It was on an eastbound Ohio & Mississippi passenger train near Seymour, Indiana.

Nature Notes

About 250,000 species of flowering plants exist on Earth today.

About one million Earths could fit into our sun.

Bad news for hay-fever sufferers: A single ragweed plant can produce a million grains of pollen a day.

One giant sequoia tree could supply enough lumber to build about 40 five-room houses.

A forest fire moves faster uphill than downhill.

Africa is the world's warmest continent.

The largest known volcano in our solar system is on Mars. Called Olympus Mons, it is 88,600 feet high—three times as tall as Mount Everest—and 335 miles across.

The largest-known iceberg, measured in 1956, was 207 miles long and 62 miles wide. That is only what showed above water. About nine-tenths of an iceberg is under water, so that was a *huge* chunk of ice!

Where in the World?

Saint Augustine, Florida, is the oldest continuously settled city in the United States. It was established in 1565 by a Spanish sailor named Pedro Menéndez de Avilés.

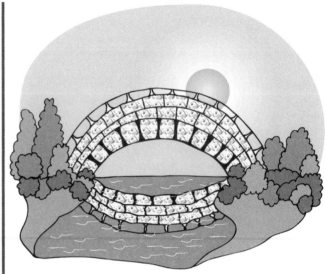

Lima, Peru, is home to the "Bridge of Eggs." The bridge, built in 1610 and still standing, was made of mortar mixed with the whites of more than 10,000 eggs.

In Brazil and China, it is considered rude to whistle.

Maine is the only U.S. state that borders just one state—New Hampshire. It also borders Canada and the Atlantic Ocean.

During the first week of a new year, by tradition, people in Korea fly kites, then release them—to carry away bad luck.

With an area of 31,820 square miles, North America's Lake Superior (one of the Great Lakes) is the largest body of freshwater in the world.

Juneau, Alaska, is the largest U.S. city in terms of land area. It covers 3,108 square miles.

The world's most active volcano, in terms of rock eruptions and lava flow, is Mount Kilauea in Hawaii. The most active volcano in terms of gas emissions is Stromboli, in Italy.

The nation of Indonesia is an archipelago composed of about 13,670 islands. More than 7,000 of those islands are uninhabited.

ANYONE HUNGRY?

If every Oreo cookie ever made were stacked one on top of the other, the stack would reach the moon and back at least six times. (More than 490 billion cookies had been produced by 2003.)

Cranberries are also called bounceberries for a good reason: A fully ripe cranberry will bounce when dropped.

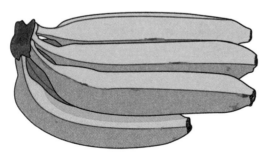

Individual bananas are called fingers. A cluster or bunch of bananas is called a hand.

As you probably know, there is no ham in a hamburger. The name comes from this popular food's origins: The first hamburgers were made in the city of Hamburg, Germany.

Americans eat about 150 million hot dogs on the 4th of July alone—and 7 billion between Memorial Day and Labor Day.

In Brazil, peas are a popular topping for pizza. In the U.S., the most popular topping is pepperoni. (We use more than 250,000 pounds of pepperoni a year as topping!)

There are 16 to 20 rows of kernels on an average ear of corn.

The first "puffed" breakfast cereal, served in colonial America, was popcorn eaten with cream and sugar.

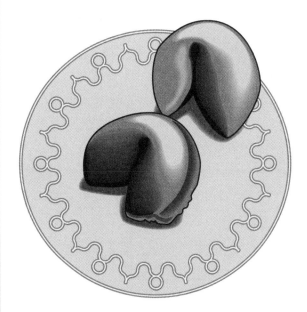

The "fortunes" that you find in Chinese cookies are inserted after they are baked—while the cookies, which harden as they cool, are still soft.

21

ANIMAL ANTICS

Q. Sharks continually replace lost teeth. About how many teeth can a shark grow in a lifetime?

A. 24,000

Q. What type of bird eats with its bill upside down?

A. the flamingo

Q. What is the only insect that can turn its head from side to side without moving its body?

A. the praying mantis, which can turn its head more than 180 degrees to either side

Q. What is the only kind of cat that can't retract its claws?

A. the cheetah

Q. What do all insects have in common?

A. six legs

Q. Do turtles have teeth?

A. No, but the edges of their jaws can be razor sharp.

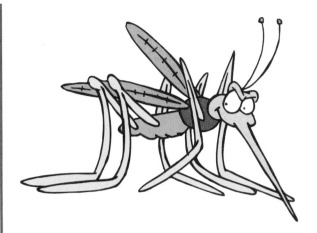

Q. Which type of mosquito bites us: the male only, the female only, or both?

A. the female only

Q. What kind of whale was Moby-Dick?

A. a sperm whale

Q. Not counting queen ants, how long is an ant's life span?

A. 8 to 10 weeks (A queen ant can live as long as 15 years.)

23

Presidents on Parade

The first wife of a president to be referred to as the First Lady was Lucy Ware Webb Hayes, in 1877. Her husband was Rutherford B. Hayes, the 19th president of the United States.

While still in office, President Ulysses S. Grant received a $20 fine for speeding—with his horse and buggy.

The Presidential Seal is set into the ceiling of the Oval Office.

Theodore Roosevelt was the first president to travel outside the U.S. during his time in office. In 1906, he went to Panama to inspect progress on the building of the Panama Canal.

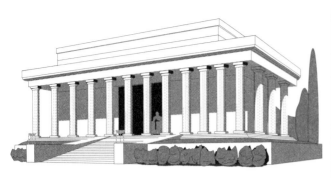

The Lincoln Memorial has 36 columns, one for each state in existence at the time of President Lincoln's death.

Founding Father presidents John Adams, Thomas Jefferson, and James Monroe all died on the 4th of July—Adams and Jefferson in 1826; Monroe in 1831.

Many historians believe that the first U.S. president to be photographed was John Quincy Adams. In 1857, James Buchanan became the first president to be photographed while taking the oath of office.

President Martin Van Buren was nicknamed the "Red Fox of Kinderhook." He also was known as the "Little Magician."

President John Quincy Adams had a pet alligator, which was kept in an East Room bathroom.

WHAT'S THE WORD?

Long ago, beds often were made of ropes stretched across wooden frames. (Sacks stuffed with straw or leaves could be laid on the ropes.) When the ropes started to stretch and sag, people used a "bed key" to wind them tighter, making the bed more comfortable. That is where we got the saying "Sleep tight!"

The letters *RSVP*, commonly used on invitations, stand for *Répondez, s'il vous plaît*—a French phrase meaning "Please respond."

Only one English word ends in *mt: dreamt.*

Ergophobia is an exaggerated or illogical fear of work. The term comes from *erg-*, a prefix meaning "work," and *phobia*, an exaggerated or illogical fear.

In the term *ZIP code*, the letters *Z–I–P* stand for Zone Improvement Plan.

Q is the least-used letter in the English alphabet.

WE'LL ALWAYS HAVE EACH OTHER!

Only two words in the English language have nothing that rhymes with them: *orange* and *silver*.

Only two common English words end in -shion: *cushion* and *fashion*.

IT'S SOME BODY!

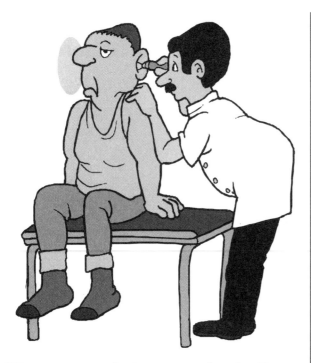

There are only two muscles in the inner ear: the stapedius and the tensor tympani. They are the smallest muscles in the human body.

In a lifetime, the average person will shed about 40 pounds of skin.

Gum disease is the most common noncontagious disease in the world.

A human's skin is thinnest on the eyelid and thickest on the sole of the foot.

A human body is made up of about 50 trillion cells.

You use about 200 muscles when you take one step forward.

During the plagues of medieval times, some European doctors recommended that patients eat garlic—and wear it around the neck—in order to stay healthy.

Information travels from your nerves to your brain at more than 200 miles per hour.

It takes more muscles to frown than to smile.

WAY BACK WHEN

The small island nation of Ceylon—now called Sri Lanka—was the first country to have a female prime minister. Sirimavo Bandaranaike served three terms: 1960-1965, 1970-1977, and 1994-2000.

Finger rings have been found from as far back as 2500 B.C., but the custom of wearing a golden wedding band did not become popular until the 16th century.

This wooden device, used to publicly punish offenders during colonial times, was called a pillory. (Stocks, a similar device, locked the offender's feet, or hands and feet.)

In 1585, Gerardus Mercator began work on a book that was the first of its type—an atlas. He died in 1594, but his son completed the work and published it the following year.

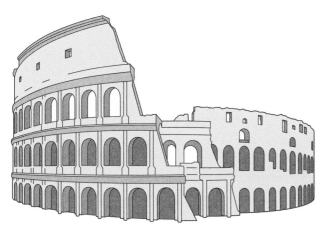

The Colosseum in Rome, which could seat about 50,000 people, was in use for about 420 years.

In 1925, the Ford Motor Company set up the first regularly scheduled airline to serve a single business. It was called the Ford Air Transport Service.

The famous Johnstown Flood, in Pennsylvania, killed 2,209 people on May 31, 1889.

At least 84 people—traveling in teams of two or more—crossed the Atlantic Ocean by plane before Charles A. Lindbergh did it in 1927. Lindbergh won international fame by making the long, hard journey solo. It took 33 1/2 hours.

The first person to cross the Brooklyn Bridge when it opened on May 24, 1883, was Emily Warren Roebling. She had helped direct the construction after her husband, chief engineer Washington Roebling, was injured. Following her across on opening day were President Chester A. Arthur, New York's Governor Grover Cleveland, and other high-ranking officials.

SPORTS STUFF

Q. Who called dribbling "one of the most spectacular and exciting maneuvers in basketball"?

A. James Naismith, the sport's founder (Dribbling was not part of his original ideas in creating the game. It developed by accident.)

Q. When was the first Kentucky Derby (horse race) run?

A. 1875

Q. In pro sports, who was known as "The Great One"?

A. Wayne Gretzky, professional ice-hockey star

Q. How many points are scored when an inner bull's-eye is hit during a darts competition?

A. 50

Q. What sport has players who are called "striker" and "sweeper?"

A. soccer

Q. In what sport are the terms *shank, slice, drive,* and *hook* used?

A. golf

Q. Walter Camp is known as the father of what sport?

A. football

Q. Which NHL player scored three goals in just 21 seconds?

A. Bill Mosienko, in 1952

Q. A disappointed fan is said to have cried out, "Say it ain't so, Joe!" to a baseball player. Who was that now-famous line for?

A. for Shoeless Joe Jackson (after the Chicago "Black Sox" scandal of 1919)

TV, Movies, Music, & More

The average American watches 120 hours of television a month.

Uncle Tom's Cabin, published in 1852, was the first American novel to sell one million copies.

The Hula-Hoop, the jigsaw puzzle, the jump rope, and the bicycle share an honor: All have been inducted into the National Toy Hall of Fame in Rochester, New York.

About 4,000 years ago, the Egyptians played a game called alquerque. Today, it is known as checkers.

In the movie version of *The Wizard of Oz*, the wizard awards one thing to each of Dorothy's three friends. To the Scarecrow, he gave a diploma representing brains; to the Tin Man, a heart-shaped watch representing a heart; and to the Cowardly Lion, a medal representing courage.

In 1987, singer Aretha Franklin—"the Queen of Soul"—became the first female inducted into the Rock and Roll Hall of Fame.

The piano was invented by Bartolomeo Cristofori of Florence, Italy, around 1709. He called his first pianolike instrument a *gravecembalo col piano e forte*, which means "harpsichord with soft and loud." By 1726, he had improved his invention, and other improvements were made later. The full name of today's 88-key instrument is *pianoforte*, which means "soft-loud."

Famous Folks

Frontiersman Daniel Boone was famous for his pioneering work *east* of the Mississippi River.

Chief Joseph, the Nez Percé tribal chief who tried to help keep his people from being forced to move to a reservation, made this now-famous statement in 1877: "I am tired; my heart is sick and sad. . . . From where the sun stands, I will fight no more forever."

Thomas Jefferson's wife, Martha, died in 1782, 19 years before he became U.S. president. During his time in office, the role of First Lady usually was filled by Dolley Madison, wife of James Madison, Jefferson's secretary of state. Jefferson's daughter also filled the role at times.

On April 7, 1940, Booker T. Washington, scientist and educator, became the first African-American to be pictured on a U.S. postage stamp. On April 5, 1956—the 100th anniversary of his birth—the house in Piedmont, Virginia, where he was born a slave, was named a U.S. National Monument.

William Shakespeare (1564–1616) is the world's most famous playwright. He died at age 51, leaving behind 37 plays as well as many sonnets and other poems.

William Henry Harrison, ninth president of the U.S., set several records. He was the last U.S. president born under British rule, the first president to die in office, and the president who served the shortest time in office—one month. Until Ronald Reagan was elected in 1980 at age 69, Harrison also was the oldest person elected to the presidency (at age 67).

The Apache warrior Goyathlay is better known by another name: Geronimo.

Marie Curie was the first person to win two Nobel Prizes. She also was the first woman ever to win the award.

John James Audubon (1785-1851) made detailed paintings of more than 4,000 species of North American birds.

ANIMAL ANTICS

A standing male red kangaroo can grow to a height of almost six feet and have a total body length (from top of head to tip of tail) of eight to nine feet.

There is a type of antelope called the *bongo*. It lives in the forests of central Africa.

The human body has about 650 muscles. A caterpillar's body has 4,000.

Compsognathus (komp-sog-NAY-thus), one of the smallest dinosaurs ever found, was the size of a chicken.

The average life span of a housefly is 10 to 21 days.

A baleen whale has no teeth. It feeds by straining seawater through hornlike bones in its mouth.

The first modern zoo was established in Vienna, Austria. The Imperial Menagerie at the Schönbrunn Palace, founded in 1752, opened in 1765. It is still in existence.

In ancient Egypt, people trained pet baboons to pick fruit from fig trees for them.

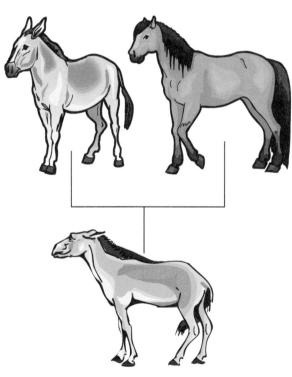

The offspring of a male donkey and a female horse is called a *mule*. When a male horse and a female donkey mate, the offspring is called a *hinny*.

Nature Notes

A rain forest averages more than 70 inches of rain a year.

The lowest temperature ever recorded in the U.S. was 78.9 degrees below zero Fahrenheit. It occurred at Prospect Creek Camp in the Endicott Mountains, Alaska, on January 23, 1971.

On February 13-19, 1959, in the greatest single snowstorm ever, 15.75 feet of snow fell at the Mount Shasta Ski Bowl in California.

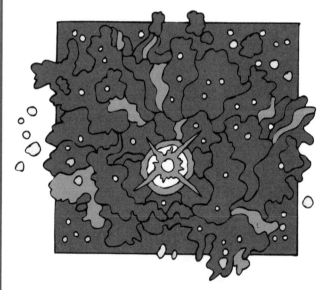

The Pistol Star, the largest star in the Milky Way, is 100 times as large as our sun. It also is 10 million times as bright.

When two full moons appear in the same month, the second one is called a blue moon. (It doesn't happen very often!)

No species of plant produces a flower that is totally black and, so far, none has been artificially created. The so-called black orchid is a very dark blue, purple, or maroon.

A car with closed windows is one of the safest places to be during a lightning storm. The electricity flows through the car's metal and into the ground.

About 5,000 earthquakes occur in Alaska each year.

IS IT STILL TODAY?

A day on Venus is about the same length as eight months on Earth. Venus turns more slowly on its axis than any other planet, making a day—one full rotation—last 243 Earth days.

The Amazing U.S.A.

From 1947 to 1969, a U.S. Air Force program called Project Blue Book investigated UFOs (unidentified flying objects).

In 1943, during World War II, copper was in short supply, so U.S. pennies were made of steel and coated with zinc instead of copper.

Alabama was the first state to proclaim Christmas a holiday, in 1836. (Christmas is the only national holiday in the U.S. that is also a religious holiday.)

The U.S. enacted its first income tax in 1874—as a result of the high cost of the Civil War.

The National Cowgirl
Hall of Fame is located in
Hereford, Texas.

The first state to ratify (approve)
the U.S. Constitution was Delaware,
on December 7, 1787.

In 1776, Benjamin Franklin, John
Adams, and Thomas Jefferson
suggested that the U.S. adopt
the Latin phrase *E Pluribus
Unum* as its motto. It means
"Out of many, one." (They got
their wish: It was adopted as the
national motto in 1782.)

In 1792, architects submitted
their designs for a presidential
residence in Washington, D.C.
James Hoban won the contest
and the right to oversee
construction of the mansion
now known as the White House.

Washington produces more
apples than any other U.S. state.

Science Fair

Q. The kinetoscope, invented in 1894 by Thomas Alva Edison, was an early version of what popular device?

A. the movie projector

Q. What do the inventors of bulletproof vests, fire escapes, and windshield wipers have in common?

A. All were women.

LOOKS PRETTY DEEP!

Q. How deep is a *fathom?*

A. six feet deep

Q. Which gives off more light: one 75-watt bulb or three 25-watt bulbs?

A. one 75-watt bulb

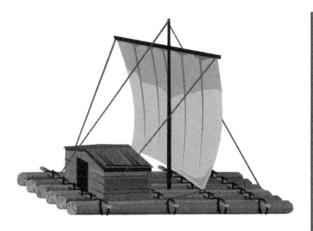

Q. Why did Thor Heyerdahl sail the *Kon-Tiki*, a raft made from local balsa wood, from Peru to Polynesia in 1947?

A. to prove that people of ancient times could have migrated the same way

Q. A *herpetologist* is a scientist who studies what?

A. reptiles

Q. Which scientist became known for the theory of relativity and for the famous formula $E = mc^2$?

A. Albert Einstein

Q. How many inventions were patented by Thomas Edison?

A. 1,093

ANYONE HUNGRY?

During World War II, some Americans used the name *liberty steak* in place of the German-sounding *hamburger*.

By law, Senate bean soup must be on the menu every day at the Capitol cafeteria in Washington, D.C.

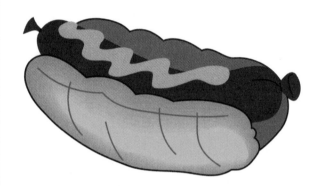

Americans consume about 20 billion hot dogs a year.

Bananas should not be stored with other fruit, because ripe bananas give off a gas that causes other fruits to ripen quickly, then rot.

More than one-fourth of all popcorn produced in the U.S. is processed in Nebraska.

Pickled ginger, minced mutton, and paneer (a form of cottage cheese) are popular pizza toppings in India.

One of the largest pumpkins ever grown weighed 1,469 pounds. Its weight was recorded October 1, 2005 at the Pennsylvania Giant Pumpkin Growers Weighoff in North Cambria, PA.

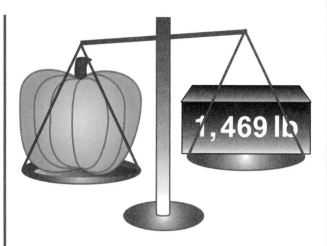

Vanilla is one of the ingredients used to make chocolate.

In 1812, First Lady Dolley Madison became the first person to serve ice cream at a presidential inaugural dinner. (The flavor she served was strawberry.)

ANIMAL ANTICS

A queen bee can lay 2,000 eggs in one day.

The longest poisonous snake is the king cobra, which grows as long as 18 feet. Its venom is powerful enough to kill an elephant.

A whistle pig is a large rodent, also known as a woodchuck or groundhog.

A cat needs one-sixth of the light a human does. Cat eyes have a layer of reflecting cells that send more light signals to its brain.

The natural color of wild goldfish is gray or greenish-brown.

In 1986, there were only 15 living California condors. Due to conservation efforts, about 200 are alive today.

A cow's stomach has four chambers, a bird's has three, and a rodent's has one.

A young orangutan will stay with its mother until it is six years old.

Tiger sharks have been found with weird things in their bellies, including boat cushions, an alarm clock, and a barrel of nails!

Where in the World?

I'M TUCKED IN, SAFE AND SOUND.

Unlike the other four Great Lakes, Lake Michigan lies entirely within the U.S. (The others border Canada and the U.S.)

The longest mountain range on Earth is the Mid-Atlantic Ridge, which is about 10,000 miles long. It lies under the Atlantic Ocean, running along the sea floor from Iceland to near the Antarctic Circle.

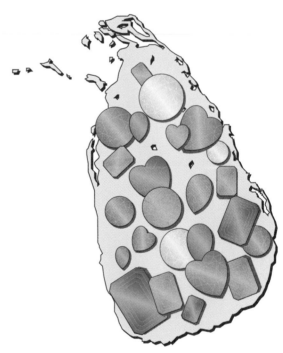

In the deserts of the southwestern U.S., more people die of drowning—in flash floods—than of thirst.

The island nation of Sri Lanka is known as Gem Island because so many valuable gemstones are found there.

KAUAI
NIIHAU
OAHU
MOLOKAI
MAUI
LANAI
KAHOOLAWE
HAWAII
HAWAII

HEY! WHERE DID WE GO?

Bermuda
Florida
Puerto Rico

The Hawaiian Islands were originally known as the Sandwich Islands. They were named for England's Earl of Sandwich—the same person the food item was named after.

More than 50 ships and 20 aircraft have disappeared in the Bermuda Triangle. Three points of land form the triangle: Bermuda, Puerto Rico, and southeast Florida (the city of Melbourne).

Australia's deserts make up the world's second-largest desert region in area. Asia's Gobi Desert is the largest.

Damascus, Syria, is probably the oldest continuously inhabited city still in existence. Archaeologists have found evidence of a city there from the third millennium B.C.

SPORTS STUFF

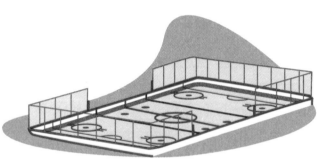

The first artificial ice-hockey rink in North America was built in New York City. It opened on February 12, 1879, in the original Madison Square Garden.

During World War II, the Pittsburgh Steelers and the Philadelphia Eagles merged into a football team called the Steagles.

In May 1984, the Chicago White Sox and the Milwaukee Brewers took the longest time ever to complete a major-league baseball game. They played 17 innings on May 8, stopped for the night, then resumed play the next day for another 8 innings before the White Sox won it, 7-6. Total playing time for that two-day game: 8 hours, 6 minutes.

Riding on just the front wheels of a skateboard is called a nose wheelie.

The first American known to take part in the sport of surfing was George Freeth. He rode the waves at Redondo Beach, California, in 1907.

IT'S TIME TO RETIRE.

In a major-league game, the average baseball lasts for six pitches. (Each major-league game starts with a supply of six dozen balls.)

Rocky Marciano was the only heavyweight boxing champion to retire without losing a professional fight. He won 49 fights, lost none.

The custom of carrying the Olympic Flame from Greece to the Games' site by Torch Relay began in 1936, for the Games held in Berlin, Germany.

The Buffalo Bills played in the Super Bowl four years in a row (1991–1994)—and lost all four times!

WAY BACK WHEN

Q. Why were the mummies of pharaohs (kings of ancient Egypt) often buried in boats?

A. The people of ancient Egypt believed that the boats would carry the pharaohs into the afterlife.

Q. How fast did the original Wright brothers' plane fly?

A. 30 miles per hour

Q. Surgeons in the 17th century performed bloodletting and tooth extraction. What other service did they offer?

A. They gave haircuts.

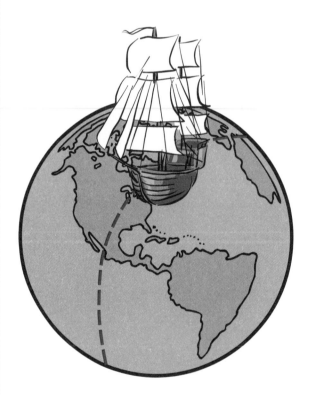

Q. How long did it take Sir Francis Drake to sail around the world?

A. 34 months (December 1577 to September 1580)

Q. What device did Christopher Columbus use on his voyages to measure the passage of time?

A. a sandglass (also called an hourglass)

Q. Before the United Nations moved to its permanent home in New York City in 1951-1952, where was its headquarters?

A. in Lake Success, New York

Q. George IV, king of England from 1820 to 1830, ordered a pair of boots to fit each of his feet. What was unusual about that?

A. Before then, each shoe was designed to be interchangeable, fitting both the right and left foot.

Q. In what country did the windmill originate, in about A.D. 644?

A. Persia (now Iran)

Science Fair

The venom from a poison-arrow frog acts as a painkiller that is 200 times better at fighting pain than morphine, a drug used in hospitals.

A space capsule re-entering Earth's atmosphere travels at about 18,000 to 25,000 miles per hour.

ARPANET was one of the first computer networks and the forerunner of today's Internet. It was established in 1969 by the Advanced Research Projects Agency (ARPA) of the U.S. Department of Defense.

The tiny dots that make up the picture on a TV or computer screen are called *pixels.*

Willis Haviland Carrier (1876–1950) invented the modern air-conditioning system.

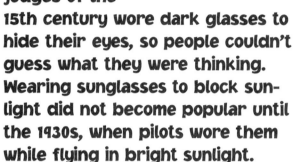

Sunglasses were invented in ancient China. Chinese judges of the 15th century wore dark glasses to hide their eyes, so people couldn't guess what they were thinking. Wearing sunglasses to block sunlight did not become popular until the 1930s, when pilots wore them while flying in bright sunlight.

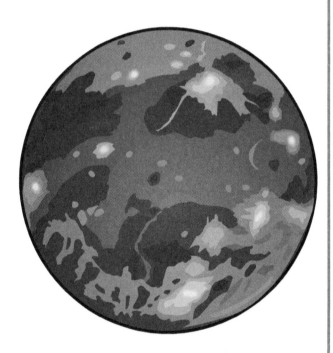

Ganymede, one of Jupiter's moons, is the largest moon in our solar system. It is larger than the planets Mercury and Pluto.

WHAT A LOAD!

The average suit of armor worn by knights during medieval times weighed 45 to 55 pounds.

THIS and THAT

Canadians celebrate Thanksgiving Day on the second Monday in October.

The base of Egypt's Great Pyramid covers 571,158 square feet—larger than the area of 13 football fields.

Before the 1920s, the color pink—now considered a girl's color—was associated with boys.

The first modern chain store was the Great Atlantic & Pacific Tea Company, founded in 1859. Later, it was known as the A & P.

There are 35 bathrooms in the White House.

The world's largest Easter egg is a sculpture that is 25.7 feet long and 18.3 feet wide. To see it, you will have to go to Vegreville in Alberta, Canada.

The world's first speed limit for cars, set in London, England, in 1903, was 20 miles per hour.

The proper name of the *Mona Lisa*, Leonardo da Vinci's famous painting, is *La Gioconda*.

Cinderella's two mean stepsisters were named Anastasia and Drizella.

Famous Folks

A popular version of Pocahontas's story is that she married John Smith, the man whose life she asked her father to spare. In real life, however, she married a different English settler—John Rolfe.

George Armstrong Custer is often referred to as "General Custer," but when he was killed at the Battle of the Little Bighorn in 1876, his military rank was lieutenant colonel. (He became a brigadier general in 1862, during the Civil War, but was court-martialed and suspended in 1867. After a year, he returned to military service with a lower rank.)

Harriet Tubman, a runaway slave, is probably the most famous "conductor" on the Underground Railroad.

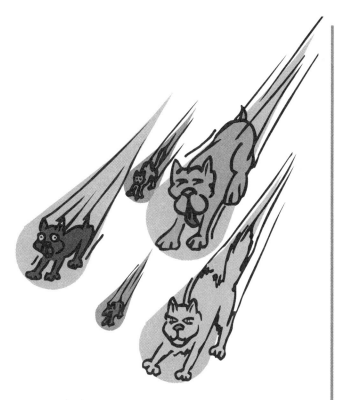

Jonathan Swift, best known as the author of *Gulliver's Travels*, was the first writer known to use the phrase "raining cats and dogs" (in 1738).

On July 20, 1969, U.S. astronaut Neil Armstrong became the first human to set foot on the moon.

Gertrude Ederle was the first woman ever honored by a ticker-tape parade in New York City. The parade celebrated her 1926 feat of being the first woman to swim across the English Channel from France to England.

One of the youngest people to receive the Nobel Peace Prize was Martin Luther King Jr. (at age 35, in 1964).

Nature Notes

Q. Is it the youngest or oldest mountains that are the roundest and lowest?

A. the oldest

Q. Diamond is the hardest mineral. What is the second hardest?

A. corundum, which is the mineral name for ruby and sapphire

Q. If all the water in Earth's atmosphere fell as rain at the same time, about how deep would it be worldwide?

A. close to one inch (0.98 inch)

Q. What type of rock can float in water?

A. pumice

Q. If all the dry land on Earth was divided equally, about how much would each person get?

A. six acres

Q. Which provides more heat when burned: a pound of wood or a pound of coal?

A. a pound of coal

Q. Which planet in our solar system has a huge revolving storm known as the Great Red Spot?

A. Jupiter

Q. What was the most rain ever to fall in a 24-hour period?

A. 73.5 inches, on March 15-16, 1952, at Chilaos, Réunion, an island in the Indian Ocean

ANIMAL ANTICS

A one-and-one-half-pound lobster is about nine years old. A lobster's age is roughly its weight multiplied by four, plus three years.

Lions are the only type of cat that lives in groups.

A spider's body has two segments; an insect's body has three.

Experts say that dinosaurs are not extinct. They remain on Earth in the form of their descendants, birds.

A group of baboons is
called a troop.

One type of oyster, the *Ostrea
edulis*, can change from male to
female with the seasons or
changes in water temperature.
Most oysters, however, are either
male or female.

The Gaboon viper, which is
poisonous, has the longest
fangs of any snake—up to
2 inches long. Its body is
up to 7 feet long.

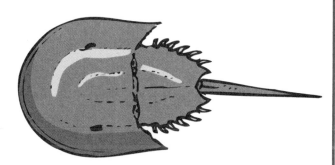

Horseshoe crabs living today
look the same as those living
300 million years ago!

Dinosaur bones have been found
all over the planet—including
Antarctica, which was not always
as cold as it is today.

TV, Movies, Music, & More

Gunsmoke holds the record for longest-running scripted series on TV. It debuted in 1955 and aired for 20 years.

Charlotte's Web, by E. B. White, is the best-selling children's book of all time.

The story of Cinderella is thought to be the best-known fairy tale in the world. It has a long history: It first appeared in China during the ninth century.

Billy Joel's *52nd Street* was the first commercially released music CD. It was released in Japan in 1982.

The song "White Christmas" was introduced in 1942 in a movie called *Holiday Inn.*

Comedy star Lucille Ball and her infant son, Desi Arnaz Jr., appeared on the cover of the first issue of *TV Guide* magazine, published in April 1953.

The first Academy Awards® presentations were made in 1927, and first broadcast on television in 1952.

Adjusting for inflation, *Cleopatra* (1963) was the most expensive movie ever made. Its budget of $44 million would amount to more than $300 million today. (*Titanic* cost about $200 million to make.)

The character named Luke Skywalker was introduced in *Star Wars*, a movie released in 1977.

The femur *(FEE-mur)*—the long bone in your thigh—is the longest and heaviest bone in the human body. It is stronger than concrete or steel!

The right lung takes in more air than the left. That is because the right lung has three lobes, while the left has only two. The left side is smaller, because it shares space with the heart.

There are four basic types of human blood: A, B, AB, and O. Type O is most common worldwide.

House dust is made of tiny fabric fuzzies; particles of mold, food, and plants; and even you—tiny bits of your dead, flaked-off skin.

Women have a sharper sense of smell than men have.

A sneeze can reach a top speed of about 100 miles per hour!

Your hair and fingernails grow faster in summer than they do in winter.

You were born color-blind—everyone is. (We are like that till we are about four months old.)

Food makes it to your stomach even if you are eating upside down.

WHAT'S THE WORD?

Q. What does a *mnemonic (nih-MAH-nik) device* help you do?

A. It helps you remember something. (*Mnemonic* comes from a Greek word meaning "to remember.")

Q. Which one of these terms is used to define the entire universe? (a) ectoplasm; (b) macrocosm; (c) microcosm; (d) plasma.

A. b (from Greek words *makro-*, which means "large" or "on a wide scale," and *kosmos*, meaning "world.")

Q. Which of these is an example of a *palindrome*: (a) *dark* and *light*; (b) Madam, I'm Adam; (c) *stile* and *style*; (d) When will Winnie wake?

A. b (A *palindrome* is a word or sentence that is spelled the same way backward and forward.)

Q. *E* is the most commonly used letter in the English language. What is the second most commonly used?

A. T

Q. The aardvark is the first animal listed in the dictionary. What is the last animal listed?

A. zyzzyva (a tropical weevil)

Q. About how many Amerindian (Native American) languages are still spoken in the U.S.?

A. 175 (Only 20 Amerindian languages are widely used. About 55 may soon disappear, as they are used by just a few elderly speakers.)

Q. Where does the term *second string*, meaning "replacement" or "backup," come from?

A. It comes from archery. During the Middle Ages, archers carried an extra string in case the one on their bow broke.

Q. If you have *musophobia*, you have an illogical or exaggerated fear of what?

A. mice (This fear is also called *murophobia* and *suriphobia*.)

Q. What does the word *hippopotamus* mean?

A. "river horse" (from the Greek word *hippopotamos—hippos* meaning "horse" and *potamos* meaning "river")

71

SPORTS STUFF

The first time a catcher's mask was used in a baseball game was in 1876, during a game played at Harvard University.

Only one major-league baseball pitcher has thrown two consecutive no-hitters: Johnny Vander Meer of the Cincinnati Reds. He accomplished that amazing feat on June 11 and June 15, 1938.

The largest crowd ever to attend a soccer match was at a World Cup game between Brazil and Uruguay. On July 16, 1950, 199,854 people packed Rio de Janeiro's Maracana Stadium for the big event.

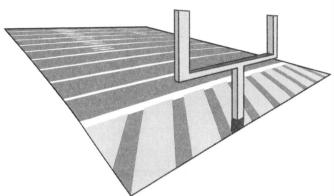

In football, the area between the 20-yard line and the goal line is called the red zone.

Sandy Koufax called pitching "the art of instilling fear." Hitters found the lefty Dodgers pitcher scary enough to get him inducted into the Hall of Fame in 1972.

Modern Olympic winners receive gold, silver, or bronze medals. Winners in the ancient Olympic Games were awarded wreaths made of laurel, wild olive, or palm leaves.

When softball was first invented in 1887, it was known by several names, including diamond ball, indoor–outdoor, mush ball, playground ball, and kitten ball.

Tennis superstar Martina Navratilova has won 167 singles titles and 165 doubles titles. Among those many victories are 20 Wimbledon titles—a record.

THIS and THAT

When people first used telephones, the usual greeting was "Are you there?" That was changed by Thomas Alva Edison. In a rush one day, he picked up the phone and shouted, "Hello!"

The base on which the Statue of Liberty sits is a star with 11 points.

In the U.S., Canada, and Great Britain, twins are born in 1 out of every 83.4 births.

The original model of the starship *Enterprise*, used in filming the first *Star Trek* TV series, is on display at the National Air and Space Museum in Washington, D.C.

On average, a person dreams about two hours each night.

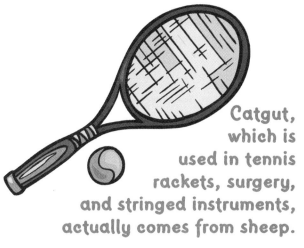

Catgut, which is used in tennis rackets, surgery, and stringed instruments, actually comes from sheep.

Among other pets, President Calvin Coolidge had a wallaby, bobcat, and pygmy hippopotamus.

The term *rock 'n' roll* was popularized by Alan Freed (1921–1965), who was a disc jockey in Cleveland, Ohio.

Pirates—and many other seamen of the time—wore earrings to prevent seasickness. They believed that pressure on the earlobe is what did the trick. (Today, some people wear special bracelets that put pressure on the wrist, for the same reason.)

The Amazing U.S.A.

Iolani Palace in Honolulu, Hawaii—former home of Hawaiian kings and queens—is the only royal palace in the United States.

About 40 percent of Americans are descended from someone who arrived through Ellis Island in New York Harbor.

"G.I. Joe" was a nickname given to U.S. soldiers during World War II. The *G.I.* was short for the words "government issue."

King's College had only eight students when it opened in New York City in 1754. Today, it has more than 23,000 students and is known as Columbia University.

Boston, Massachusetts, was the first city in the U.S. to have a subway (underground rail system). It opened on September 1, 1897.

In addition to the six types of coins still issued today (pennies, nickels, dimes, quarters, half dollars, and dollars), the U.S. Mint once issued six other types of coins. They were a half-cent, a two-cent, a three-cent made of silver, a three-cent made of nickel, a half-dime, and a twenty-cent.

New Jersey has more hazardous-waste sites than any other U.S. state. (It had 113 in 2003.)

The first public reading of the Declaration of Independence, given by Colonel John Nixon, took place outside the State House in Philadelphia, Pennsylvania, on July 8, 1776.

Did you know that some states have an official beverage? Ohio's is tomato juice. Florida's is orange juice.

ANIMAL ANTICS

Ferrets, weasels, minks, badgers, otters, wolverines, and skunks belong to the mustelidae family of animals. (All can give off a strong musky odor when disturbed.)

The bald eagle is not really bald. It has dark-brown body feathers, with a white head and tail feathers. That pale head makes it look bald from a distance.

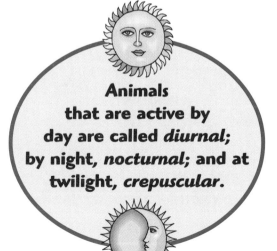

Animals that are active by day are called *diurnal*; by night, *nocturnal*; and at twilight, *crepuscular*.

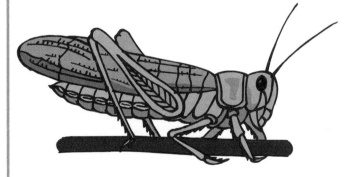

As the temperature rises, a cricket's chirps speed up.

A group of turtles is called a *bale* or a *turn*.

The word *dinosaur* means "terrifying lizard."

In 1879, the city fathers of Liege, Belgium, tried to train cats to deliver mail from the central post office to outlying villages. It didn't work.

The elephant, which has only two kneecaps, is the only animal with four legs that bend in the same direction.

The cockatiel is the most popular breed of pet bird in the U.S. The rest of the top five, in order, are the parakeet, the finch, the parrot, and the lovebird.

Where in the World?

Q. What country's name, in its people's own language, means "central glorious people's united country"?

A. China

Q. Where in the U.S. can you find a replica of the famous Parthenon in Greece?

A. Nashville, Tennessee

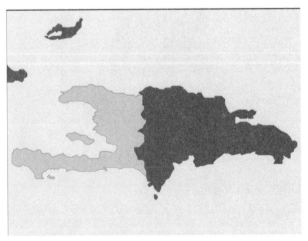

Q. At what height is a hill usually considered to be a mountain?

A. There is no rule or standard about this—it depends on what is nearby. A mountain is a landform that is significantly higher than the surrounding area.

Q. What independent countries make up the island of Hispaniola?

A. the Dominican Republic and Haiti

NEW ZEALAND

Q. What is the capital of New Zealand?

A. Wellington (It was named in honor of Arthur Wellesley, the first duke of Wellington, who was a hero of Britain's war against Napoleon.)

Q. In which U.S. state would you find Crater Lake?

A. Oregon

Q. Which of these island nations is *not* in the Indian Ocean: Comoros, Fiji, Maldives, Seychelles?

A. Fiji, which is in the South Pacific Ocean

Q. How many time zones does Alaska have?

A. two (Before 1983, it had four.)

Pyramid of the Sun

Q. In 1884, archaeologists began unearthing a great ancient city dominated by a massive structure called the Pyramid of the Sun. The pyramid is 216 feet tall, with a base covering nearly 10 acres. Where is it?

A. The city—called Teotihuacán (tay-oh-tee-wah-KAHN), City of the Gods—is in Mexico.

WAY BACK WHEN

San Francisco's Golden Gate Bridge opened to the public in 1937.

García López de Cárdenas of Spain was the first European to see the Grand Canyon. He was part of a team led by Francisco Vázquez de Coronado, a famous explorer.

Switzerland remained neutral during both World War I and World War II.

The Taíno (also called the Arawak, or the Antillean Arawak) was the first Native American tribe Christopher Columbus met in 1492.

AUGUST

S M T W T F S

The month of August was named after Augustus Caesar, the first Roman emperor.

The first secretary general of the United Nations was Trygve Lie, of Norway. He served from 1946 to 1952.

Mother's Day became a U.S. national holiday in 1914.

Europe's Hundred Years' War lasted 116 years (1337–1453).

The first automobile race in the U.S., held on November 28, 1895, was won by J. Frank Duryea. It took him 10 hours to travel the 54 miles to the finish line. Six cars left Chicago at 8:55 a.m. Duryea reached Evanston, Illinois, just after 7 p.m. Only one other car finished the race, arriving about 9 p.m.

Nature Notes

HEY, IT'S BEEN A WHILE. HERE I COME!

The record for having the longest period without rain goes to Arica, Chile. It lasted 14 years, from October 1903 to January 1918. Arica isn't the only dry spot in Chile. Chile's Atacama Desert—the driest place on Earth—gets an average of just 0.0003 inch of rain a year.

Poison oak is not related to oak trees, and poison ivy is not a true ivy. Both poison oak and poison ivy are in the cashew family.

A storm is not considered a hurricane until the wind's speed is 74 miles per hour or faster.

Bats are the only mammals that fly.

Acid rain is what forms when industrial pollution mixes with rain. Acid rain can be as acidic as lemon juice—more than 10 times as acidic as normal rain.

Earth is the only planet in our solar system not named for an ancient god. Mercury, Venus, Mars, Jupiter, Saturn, Neptune, and Pluto were named after gods of the ancient Romans. Uranus was named for the ancient Greeks' god of the sky.

Saturn is not the only planet in our solar system that has rings. Recent space probes have found that Jupiter, Uranus, and Neptune also have rings.

Earth takes 365.242 days to make one complete orbit of the sun. Round that off, and you get 365.25 days. That one quarter of a day is why we have leap years. Every four years, we add a day to February, which keeps our calendars in sync with Mother Nature.

THIS and THAT

California has more operating roller coasters than any other U.S. state.

Dolls are probably the oldest known plaything.

100000000000000000000000000000000000000000

A *googol* is the number 1 followed by 100 zeroes.

On an average weekday, two billion telephone calls are made in the U.S.

The Leaning Tower of Pisa was built to serve as a bell tower.

Groundhog Day is celebrated on February 2 in the U.S. and Canada. The tradition of having a rodent "predict" the start of spring was brought to the Americas by German immigrants. A badger was their original forecasting animal.

The International Museum of Cartoon Art, the only museum in the world devoted only to cartoons, is located in Boca Raton, Florida.

Mr. Potato Head was the first toy ever advertised on network TV (in 1952).

The best-selling musical instrument in the world is the harmonica.

SPORTS STUFF

Charles Cooper was the first African-American basketball player to be drafted into the NBA. He was tapped by the Boston Celtics in 1950.

Babe Ruth and Hank Aaron scored the same number of runs in their illustrious careers: 2,174.

The first officially recognized professional football game was played in Latrobe, Pennsylvania, on August 31, 1895.

The first baseball player to earn $1,000,000 a year was Nolan Ryan, with the Houston Astros, in 1980.

The first pro hockey player to score 50 goals in one season was Maurice Richard, during the 1944–1945 season. (That feat was not matched till Bobby Hull did it in 1961–1962.)

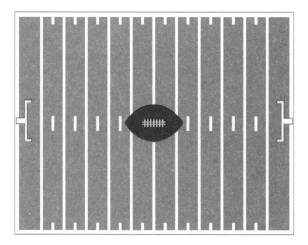

A football field is 120 yards long (including end zones) and 160 feet wide.

The first baseball game using rules organized by Alexander Cartwright was played on June 19, 1846, in Hoboken, New Jersey.

Girls started playing on Little League baseball teams in 1974.

Whale-skin eating, ear weight-lifting, and the seal hop are among the events at the annual Eskimo-Indian Olympics.

ANYONE HUNGRY?

Q. Which part of a strawberry plant is the fruit?

A. Those tiny things on a strawberry's skin that we think of as seeds are the plant's actual fruits.

Q. Popcorn, which is native to the Western Hemisphere, has been eaten by Native Americans for centuries. How old is the oldest known popcorn kernel?

A. at least 1,000 years old

Q. What vegetable is one of the oldest known crops?

A. peas

Q. Why does honey give you energy quickly?

A. It is made of two simple sugars that give energy: glucose and fructose. The human body has to break most foods down into these sugars, but in honey, they are ready to go!

Q. What is your favorite school lunch from the cafeteria?

A. According to the American School Food Service Association, pizza is tops with U.S. schoolkids.

Q. What is the most popular fresh fruit in the U.S.?

A. Bananas. More are sold in the U.S. than any other fruit.

Q. When and where was the world's largest pizza made?

A. On December 8, 1990, in Norwood, South Africa. It measured 122 feet, 8 inches in diameter! Making it took 9,920 pounds of flour; 1,984 pounds of tomato puree; 3,968 pounds of cheese; and 198 pounds of salt.

Science Fair

Taxonomy is a system that biologists use to classify every known living organism. Taxonomic categories, from most general to most specific, are *kingdom*, *phylum*, *class*, *order*, *family*, *genus*, and *species*.

A *nanosecond* is one billionth of a second. (The prefix *nano-* means "one billionth of.") It is a measurement used by few people, other than scientists.

A *holograph* is a photo in 3-D. Instead of using a lens to focus light on a photographic plate, a holographer uses a laser beam. Parts of the beam reflect off the object and reach the photographic plate at different times, creating a three-dimensional image.

The first computer-generated weather forecast was made in 1950.

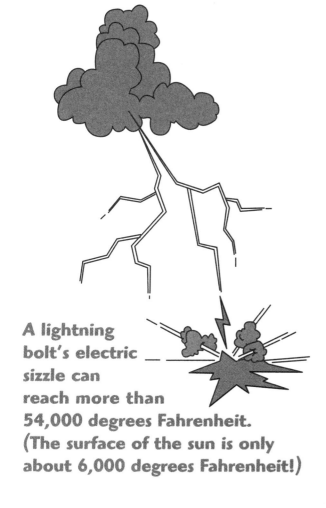

A lightning bolt's electric sizzle can reach more than 54,000 degrees Fahrenheit. (The surface of the sun is only about 6,000 degrees Fahrenheit!)

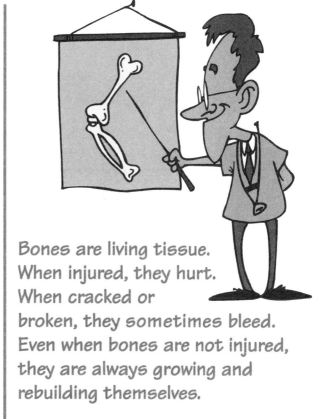

Bones are living tissue. When injured, they hurt. When cracked or broken, they sometimes bleed. Even when bones are not injured, they are always growing and rebuilding themselves.

Galileo (1564–1642) was the first person to use the magnifying power of a telescope to study objects in outer space. Until he observed the rough and rocky surface of the moon, people had believed it to be a smooth globe of light.

ENIAC was the first all-electronic, digital, main-frame computer. (ENIAC stands for Electronic Numerical Integrator and Calculator.) Invented in 1946, ENIAC was far faster than any computing machine ever built before, but it filled a 30-by-50-foot room and weighed 30 tons.

93

Famous Folks

The first human to orbit Earth was Yuri A. Gagarin, a Russian cosmonaut, on April 12, 1961. Gagarin's spacecraft, *Vostok 1*, traveled at an average altitude of 187 miles above Earth. The once-around-the-planet trip took 1 hour and 48 minutes.

In 1932, Amelia Earhart became the first woman to fly solo across the Atlantic Ocean. She made the Newfoundland-to-Ireland flight in record time: 14 hours, 56 minutes.

Five of the ten richest people in the world belong to the Walton family. Their wealth was left to them by Sam Walton, who founded Wal-Mart in 1962. Sam died in 1992. His widow and four children are worth about $20 billion each.

The first woman to run for president of the United States was Victoria Woodhull, in 1872. A well-known speaker on women's rights, Woodhull called for American women to be allowed to vote—a right not granted until 1920.

King Henry VIII of England had six wives—three of whom were named Catherine. His wives, in order, were Catherine of Aragon, Anne Boleyn, Jane Seymour, Anne of Cleves, Catherine Howard, and Catherine Parr.

Though Christopher Columbus is credited with "discovering" America, he saw very little of it. Most of his explorations were on small Caribbean islands. He also landed on what today are Honduras, Nicaragua, and Venezuela, but he didn't travel far.

Simón Bolívar is known as the George Washington of South America. He led—and won—a long struggle to free his homeland of Venezuela from Spanish rule. Under Bolívar's leadership, independence was also won for Bolivia, Colombia, Ecuador, Panama, and Peru.

When J. K. Rowling sent out her first Harry Potter book, many publishers turned it down. Finally, one company, Bloomsbury, took a chance and published it in 1997. It was a huge and immediate success. By 2004, Rowling's Harry Potter book series had raised her to the rank of billionaire. She is the first author to reach the billion-dollar mark in personal worth.

ANIMAL ANTICS

People used to think that a dog eating grass was a sign that it was going to rain. But all it really means is that the dog feels like eating grass! (That is okay as long as the grass hasn't been fertilized with harmful chemicals.)

A rat can't go more than 48 hours without water. When thirsty, it will chew through almost anything to get to it!

The great bustard is the world's heaviest bird. It weighs up to 40 pounds and has a wingspan of about 8 feet. It can fly if it has to, but mostly it lives on the ground.

Having trouble getting your dog to swallow medicine? Put the pill on the back of its tongue, then blow in its nose.

In the U.S., more than 100 million birds a year die by crashing into windows.

Polar bears in the wild eat birds, caribou, fish, grass, and seaweed—even a stranded whale now and then. But seals are their favorite food.

Fish cough.

Nearly half of an ostrich's height is in its neck.

Bullfighters don't have to use a red cape to anger a bull—the animal is color-blind.

PRESIDENTS ON PARADE

Q. Which First Lady was responsible for the planting of thousands of Japanese cherry trees around the Tidal Basin in Washington, D.C.?

A. Helen Herron Taft, wife of President William Howard Taft, in 1912

Q. Who was the first U.S. president to win a Nobel Prize?

A. Theodore Roosevelt, who was awarded the Nobel Peace Prize in 1906

Q. Harry S. Truman was the 33rd U.S. president. What did the *S* in his name stand for?

A. Nothing. His parents couldn't decide between his two grand-fathers' names, Shippe and Solomon, so they just used an *S*.

Q. Who was the first U.S. president to die while still in office?

A. William Henry Harrison (of illness, after only one month in office)

98

Q. Who was the only U.S. president to have been a POW (prisoner of war)?

A. Andrew Jackson. He was only 14 when he was taken prisoner during the American Revolution.

Q. Which U.S. president wrote a Pulitzer Prize–winning book, called *Profiles in Courage*, and was honored as a World War II hero?

A. John F. Kennedy

Q. Weighing more than 300 pounds, who was the heaviest president in U.S. history?

A. William Howard Taft

Q. Who was the first U.S. president born in a log cabin?

A. Andrew Jackson, born in 1767 (James A. Garfield, born in 1831, was the last.)

Where in the World?

At the Crater of Diamonds State Park in Murfreesboro, Arkansas, anyone who pays a fee can dig for gemstones and keep whatever is found. It is the only public-use diamond mine in the world.

The city of Pittsburgh, Pennsylvania, has more than 720 bridges.

The world's largest St. Patrick's Day parade is not held in Ireland. It takes place in New York City.

Mount Everest was named for Sir George Everest (1790-1866), a Welsh surveyor. Until 1865, when the world's tallest mountain was renamed in Sir George's honor, it was known as Peak XV.

Mainland Australia is the only continent with no active volcanoes. (Two active volcanoes can be found on islands that are Australian territory.)

Water from all five Great Lakes flows into the Atlantic Ocean by a single waterway—the St. Lawrence River and Seaway.

Russia is the largest country in land area.

The official state bird of Hawaii is the nene (NAY-nay)—also called the Hawaiian goose.

IT'S SOME BODY!

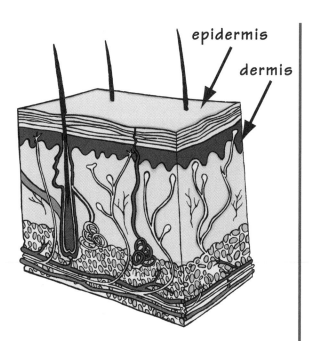

epidermis

dermis

Humans have two layers of skin: the epidermis (outer layer) and the dermis (inner layer).

Blonds have more hair per square inch than redheads and brunettes have.

Your lips have no sweat glands.

About 75 percent of the human brain is water.

About 10 percent of the world's population is left-handed.

The average person drinks about 16,000 gallons of water in a lifetime.

The human body must burn 3,500 calories to work off a single pound of fat.

The average human heart, at rest, can pump about 5.3 quarts of blood per minute.

Nature Notes

Water vapor, hydrogen, and dust are all major components of clouds.

Under the best viewing conditions, about 3,000 stars can be seen with the naked eye.

The coconut is the largest plant seed on Earth.

About 20 percent of Earth's surface is covered by warm desert.

The lowest temperature ever recorded in the Sahara Desert was 5 degrees Fahrenheit.

One inch of rain equals 10 inches of snow in water content.

With an average of 106 days of heavy fog a year, Cape Disappointment, Washington, is the foggiest place in the U.S.

Ninety percent of the world's ice is found in Antarctica.

Sunflowers really do follow the sun—as buds. When sunflowers are in the bud stage, the buds turn to face the sun as it moves from east to west. After the flowers bloom, however, they face east.

THIS and THAT

Each year, Americans throw away enough disposable diapers to stretch from here to the moon and back several times.

Men and women started wearing shoe styles that were different from each other in the 18th century. Before then, men's and women's shoes were the same.

Here is a truly "shocking" fact: A park ranger named Roy C. Sullivan was struck by lightning—and survived—a record seven times between 1942 and 1977.

106

Most experts believe that the earliest tattoos are the ones found on Egyptian and Nubian mummies dating from about 2000 B.C.

One ounce of gold can be pounded into a thin sheet covering 187 square feet.

Chewing gum while peeling or slicing onions will help keep your eyes from tearing.

The ancient Romans loved luxurious baths. Wealthy men were known to bathe in wine and wealthy women in milk.

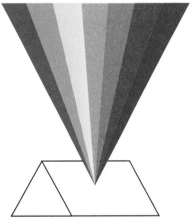

The seven colors in the light spectrum always appear in the same order: red, orange, yellow, green, blue, indigo, and violet. To remember this, imagine someone named Roy G. Biv. Each letter of that name is the first letter of those seven colors, in order.

The Amazing U.S.A.

Q. How long is the term of a U.S. senator?

A. six years

Q. Who was the first American woman to walk in space?

A. *Challenger* astronaut Kathryn Sullivan, in October 1984

Q. The nickname "Old Glory" refers to what?

A. the U.S. flag

Q. Who was America's first known female soldier?

A. Deborah Sampson (during the American Revolution)

Q. About how many Native Americans live in the U.S. today?

A. two million (About one-third of them live on reservations.)

108

Q. What was the first colony in North America to outlaw slavery?

A. Rhode Island (on May 18, 1652)

Q. After the original 13 colonies, what was the next state to enter the Union?

A. Vermont (on March 4, 1791)

Q. Robert E. Lee was the third-ranking officer in the Confederate Army. Who was the first?

A. Samuel Cooper

Q. Which state has a law on its books requiring every citizen to take a bath at least once a year?

A. Kentucky

SPORTS STUFF

Most wooden baseball bats are made from the wood of ash trees.

Tug-of-war was once an Olympic event.

The NFL's all-time leading rusher is Emmitt Smith. By the end of the 2005 season, he had 18,355 career yards.

The first World Cup soccer tournament was held in 1930. Uruguay's team defeated Argentina's, 4–2.

The game of hockey was originally called hurley.

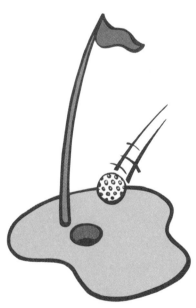

A panel of experts gave the title of Golfer of the Century (for the twentieth century) to male golfer, Jack Nicklaus, and female golfer, Mickey Wright.

Frank Robinson was the first baseball player to win the Most Valuable Player award in both major leagues. He was named the National League's MVP in 1961, when he was with the Cincinnati Reds. The American League named him MVP in 1966, when he was playing for the Baltimore Orioles.

The first TV broadcast of a major-league baseball game took place on August 26, 1939. The game was between the Brooklyn Dodgers and the Cincinnati Reds. (A college baseball game, between Columbia and Princeton universities, was broadcast on May 17, 1939.)

Joe Montana, quarterback of the San Francisco 49ers, was the first football player to win the Super Bowl MVP award three times—in 1982, 1985, and 1990.

ANIMAL ANTICS

A pigeon's bones weigh less than its feathers.

With a record weight of more than 2,000 pounds, the leatherback sea turtle is the world's largest turtle.

Most spiders have eight eyes, but some have six, or four, or fewer.

Lions once roamed wild in North America, but they disappeared from the North American continent about 10,000 years ago.

Snakes do not have ears. They "hear" by sensing vibrations through the jawbone, which sends signals through connecting bones to the inner ear and brain.

An adult male flamingo is three to five feet tall. Female flamingos are slightly shorter.

The mako shark has been clocked at a speed of 43 miles per hour, making it the fastest swimmer of all sharks.

There are about 170,000 different kinds of butterflies and moths.

The ocean sunfish (also called the mola or the headfish) produces more eggs at one time than any other kind of fish—up to 300,000,000.

TV, Movies, Music, & More

There are 64 squares
on a chessboard.

In 1953, an unknown singer named Elvis Presley paid $3.98 to record two songs to his mother: "My Happiness" and "That's When Your Heartaches Begin."

Theodor Geisel, better known as Dr. Seuss, wrote *Green Eggs and Ham* after an editor challenged him to write a book using fewer than 50 different words.

It is possible to deal 2,598,960 different five-card poker hands from a 52-card deck.

Bram Stoker set his famous novel *Dracula* in Transylvania—a real place in Europe that he had never visited.

Snoopy, the famous comic-strip beagle, was born at the Daisy Hill Puppy Farm.

Author L. Frank Baum named *Oz* after a filing-cabinet drawer in his office. One was labeled "A–N"; the other, "O–Z."

A CAST OF THOUSANDS

The Academy Award®–winning movie *Gandhi*, directed by Richard Attenborough, used hundreds of thousands of extras—the most ever used in a film. More than 300,000 extras appear in the funeral scene alone.

Arthur Wynne, an English journalist, created the first crossword puzzle known to be published. His puzzle ran in the *New York World* newspaper on December 21, 1913.

Science Fair

The largest constellation in the sky is Hydra, also known as the Water Snake, the Sea Serpent, or the Water Monster.

Nylon was the first completely synthetic material ever made. On "N" Day—May 15, 1940—nylon's inventor, DuPont, began selling stockings made with nylon, and sold 780,000 pairs in one day.

If the diameter of Earth were 10 percent smaller, all life would freeze.

In areas that are sunny most of the year, solar energy—collected by special panels—can be an efficient, nonpolluting energy source.

Galileo Galilei invented the thermometer to measure air temperature, in about 1592.

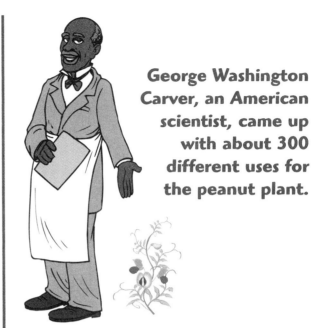

George Washington Carver, an American scientist, came up with about 300 different uses for the peanut plant.

Earth orbits the sun at about 66,700 miles per hour.

The technique of growing plants without soil is called hydroponics.

An accidental error in a computer program is called a *bug*. The term originated in 1945, when a malfunctioning computer at Harvard University was found to have a moth in one of its circuits.

Famous Folks

Q. The captain of the British ship *Endeavour* successfully navigated the Great Barrier Reef off the coast of Australia—one of the world's most challenging sea courses. What was his name?

A. James Cook (1728–1779)

Q. Who, in 1896, told newspaper reporters this now-famous statement: "The report of my death has been greatly exaggerated"?

A. Mark Twain, the famous author, responding to rumors that he had died

>

Q. Jane Goodall is famous for studying what kind of animals?

A. chimpanzees

Q. Helen Keller could not see, hear, or speak. What was the name of the teacher who helped her overcome her disabilities?

A. Anne Sullivan

Q. Who said, "No one can make you feel inferior without your consent"?

A. Eleanor Roosevelt

Q. Who said, "Genius is one percent inspiration, ninety-nine percent perspiration"?

A. Thomas Alva Edison, the famous inventor

Q. What did Charles Dickens, Thomas Alva Edison, and Mark Twain have in common?

A. None of them finished elementary school.

Q. Who wrote: "In spite of everything, I still believe that people are good at heart"?

A. Anne Frank (in *The Diary of Anne Frank*)

ANYONE HUNGRY?

In 1597, an English herbalist named John Gerard published *The Herball*—the first known catalogue of plants. It included a then-popular belief: that tomatoes are poisonous. Italians, Arabs, and Spaniards ate tomatoes, but few English or Americans did so until the early 19th century.

Natural vanilla flavoring comes from orchids. (Vanilla beans are the unripe fruit of certain types of tropical orchid plants.)

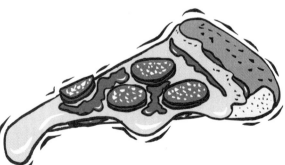

Pizza is the most popular food in the U.S.

Wheat is the world's most widely cultivated crop.

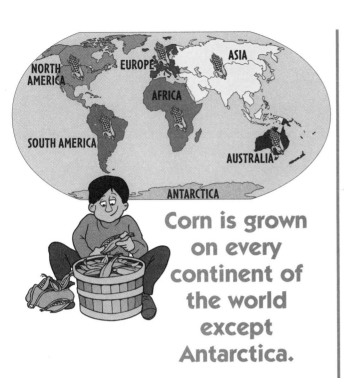

Corn is grown on every continent of the world except Antarctica.

Why wash dishes? A Taiwanese inventor has come up with plates and bowls made of oatmeal. After finishing your meal, you can eat the plate—or boil it into a paste to feed pets or farm animals!

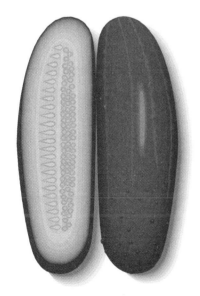

A cucumber is 96 percent water.

Monks in Germany created the pretzel in A.D. 610. Its shape was meant to represent a child's arms folded in prayer.

Americans eat a lot of chocolate—more than 11 pounds per person per year. But the U.S. is only 11th in worldwide chocolate consumption. Number one is Switzerland: more than 22 pounds per person a year!

WAY BACK WHEN

In 1744, Benjamin Franklin issued the first mail-order catalogue in the U.S.—to sell books.

The circus as we know it today came into being during the mid-1700s.

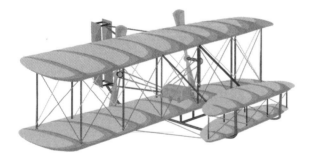

In 1908, five years after the famous first flight at Kitty Hawk, North Carolina, Wilbur Wright made his longest flight. He stayed aloft for more than 2 hours and traveled 77 miles.

Before Michelangelo created his famous paintings on the ceiling of the Vatican's Sistine Chapel, the ceiling was painted with golden stars on a blue sky.

The first shots of the Civil War were fired on April 12, 1861, at Fort Sumter, in the harbor of Charleston, South Carolina.

About one million people—one-eighth of the population—died from starvation when Ireland's potato crop failed in 1845–1850.

The first time a U.S. street was paved with asphalt was in 1870 in Newark, New Jersey.

King Kullen, the world's first supermarket, opened in the U.S. in 1930.

Alexandre-Gustave Eiffel, the man who designed Paris's Eiffel Tower, also helped build another world-famous structure: the Statue of Liberty. Frédéric-Auguste Bartholdi was the Statue's sculptor, but Eiffel helped design the framework that supports it.

WHAT'S THE WORD?

A group of crows is called a *murder*.

Every letter of the alphabet appears at least once in this sentence: *The quick brown fox jumps over the lazy dog.*

The acronym *radar* stands for "**ra**dio **d**etecting **a**nd **r**anging."

Signs with the warning CAVE CANEM were used by ancient Romans. It means "Beware the dog!"

It took Noah Webster about 17 years to compile the first American dictionary, the *American Dictionary of the English Language,* which he published in 1828.

The name *Jeep* came from the letters *GP.* At first, they were a manufacturer's abbreviation: *G* for government, *P* for a certain type of reconnaissance car. Later, they were short for "general purpose."

A *horologist* is not someone who writes or reads horoscopes. It is a person who makes or repairs clocks. (The term comes from the Greek word *hora,* meaning "hour" or "season."

A *xenophobe* (ZEH-nuh-fobe) is someone who fears foreigners. The term comes from the Greek words *xenos,* meaning "stranger," and *phobos,* meaning "fear.")

Where in the World?

Until railroads made it possible to travel long distances in a short time, every area set its own standard time. Time zones were invented to help travelers avoid schedule problems.

Mount Aconcagua *(ah-kone-KAH-gwah)*, in Argentina, is the highest point in the Western Hemisphere. It rises 22,834 feet above sea level.

More than 400 cities in the world have a population of more than 1 million.

Of all the world's continents, South America has the greatest variety of plants and animals.

There are more islands in the Pacific Ocean—about 25,000—than in all the other oceans combined.

The continent of Africa has 53 independent countries.

In the English language, only five of the world's countries have one-syllable names: Chad, France, Greece, Laos (in one of its pronunciations), and Spain.

Utah is home to the biggest man-made hole in the U.S., and one of the biggest on Earth: a copper mine near the village of Bingham Canyon.

In Matanchen Bay, Mexico, the waves are so long that a surfer can ride a single wave for more than 5,000 feet—almost a mile!

IT'S SOME BODY!

Q. Many people have a malady called *furfur*. What is it?

A. dandruff

Q. What happens to the skin of someone with a disease called *ichthyosis* (ik-thee-OH-sis)?

A. It becomes dry and scaly.

Q. Where did the expression "goose pimples" come from?

A. from how a goose's skin looks when its feathers are plucked (also called goose bumps or gooseflesh)

Q. About how many times does the average human take a breath during a 24-hour period?

A. 24,000

Q. Was the brain of a Neanderthal larger or smaller than ours?

A. larger

Q. How long does it take for blood to make a complete circuit of the human body?

A. under a minute

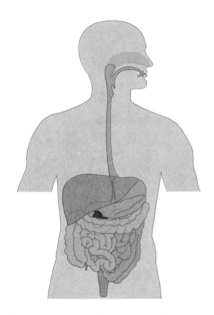

Q. About how long is the small intestine in an adult human?

A. 22 to 25 feet long

Q. If you lose the sight in one eye, how much of your vision do you lose?

A. about one fifth (but all of your depth perception)

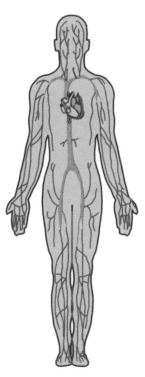

Q. How many miles of blood vessels, on average, are in the human body?

A. about 100,000 miles for an adult; about 60,000 miles for a child

Nature Notes

More water flows from the Amazon River into the ocean than from any other river in the world.

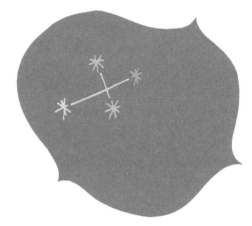

The smallest constellation is the Southern Cross—also called Crux.

A single galaxy can contain hundreds of billions of stars.

An oak tree must be at least 20 years old before it can produce acorns.

The most destructive volcanic eruption in the history of the United States was the eruption of Mount St. Helens, in Washington, in May 1980.

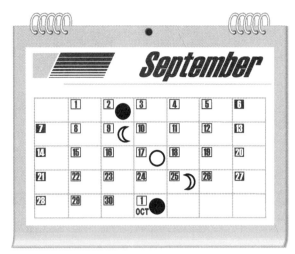

A lunar month is 29.53 days—the length of time it takes from one new moon to the next (also called lunation).

Flowering plants first appeared during the Cretaceous Period (145 to 65 million years ago).

The *cumulonimbus (KYOOM-yuh-loh-NIM-bus)* is the tallest type of cloud. It can tower from near the ground to as high as 60,000 feet—more than twice the height of Mount Everest.

The world's tallest grass, bamboo, can grow to a height of 130 feet.

A cockroach can live about a week without its head. It dies of thirst, because it can't drink water.

The capybara, which lives in Central and South America, is the world's largest rodent. It can grow to 4 feet in length and weigh 100 pounds.

Cats do not chew food the same way humans do. They use their teeth to cut through or tear up food, then they swallow it in large chunks.

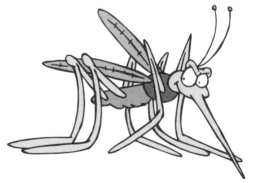

Worldwide, there are about 2,500 different mosquito species. About 150 of them live in the U.S.

The honeybee communicates by doing distinctive dances.

There are more than 20,000 species of fish.

The aardvark, whose name in the Afrikaans language means "earth pig," feeds mostly on ants and termites.

The sun bear, found in southeast Asia, is the smallest type of bear. The largest is the Kodiak bear, a type of brown bear. It is the largest living land carnivore.

An adult dog has 42 teeth.

THIS and THAT

One drop per second from a leaky faucet will waste 2,700 gallons of water in a year.

Royalties from Irving Berlin's song "God Bless America" go to the Boy Scouts and Girl Scouts of America.

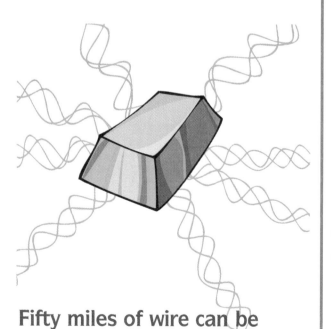

Fifty miles of wire can be made from one ounce of gold.

The Smithsonian Institution, in Washington, D.C., is the largest museum complex in the world. It has 16 separate museums and the National Zoo, as well as various research centers.

The sound of human snoring can get close to 90 decibels—about as loud as a lawn mower or chain saw.

An old Texas almanac advised that tea made by boiling an old shoe was a good cure for lumbago (backache).

King Arthur's sword had a name: Excalibur.

If you lie on your back and slowly raise your legs, you won't sink in quicksand.

In skywriting, the average letter is 1,320 feet (quarter-mile) high, and the plume of smoke is about 75 feet wide.

The Amazing U.S.A.

The first U.S. Minimum Wage Law was passed in 1938. At that time, the minimum wage was 25 cents an hour.

If the heads on Mount Rushmore had bodies, the statues would be about 500 feet tall—about as tall as a 50-story skyscraper.

Americans use about 50,000 pounds of toothpaste per day.

The first female governor in the U.S. was Nellie Tayloe Ross. In 1924, she was elected in place of her husband, Governor William Bradford Ross of Wyoming, who died while running for reelection.

EVERYONE KNOWS THAT I'M WORTH TEN CENTS!

A dime is the only U.S. coin that does not say how many cents it is worth.

Big Bend National Park, in southwestern Texas, is the only national park that runs along part of the U.S.–Mexico border. For a little more than 100 miles, it forms the U.S. side of the Rio Grande, the official border between the U.S. and Mexico.

The cadet colors at the U.S. Military Academy at West Point, New York, are black, gray, and gold. The colors represent the components of gunpowder: charcoal (black), potassium nitrate (gray), and sulfur (gold).

Benjamin Franklin was unhappy with the choice of the bald eagle as the symbol of the United States. He wanted it to be the wild turkey.

The official name of the Statue of Liberty is *Liberty Enlightening the World*.

SPORTS STUFF

Baseball manager Casey Stengel once told a player, "Kid, you're too small. You ought to go out and shine shoes." That "kid," Phil Rizzuto, stuck with baseball. He became a star shortstop for the New York Yankees, and was inducted into the Baseball Hall of Fame in 1994.

Surfing was invented hundreds of years ago by Polynesians.

ONE, TWO, THREE . . .

There are 324 to 492 dimples on a modern golf ball.

In 1986, Greg LeMond became the first non-European bicyclist—and first American—to win the 2,235-mile-long race called the Tour de France. (He also won it in 1989 and 1990.)

An official baseball weighs between 5 and 5.25 ounces.

Rickey Henderson holds the career record in pro baseball for stolen bases.

The first Wimbledon tennis tournament was held at Merton, England, in 1877.

The Harlem Globetrotters, a famous basketball team that excels in comedy as well as ball-handling skills, has been entertaining audiences since 1927.

Think it is easy for a golfer to get a hole in one? Think again: The odds are about 1 in 25,000!

TV, Movies, Music, & More

Q. In the classic Bugs Bunny cartoon *Rabbit Hood*, the Sheriff of Nottingham catches Bugs doing what?

A. taking carrots from the king's garden

Q. What was the motto of the Three Musketeers?

A. "All for one and one for all!"

Q. What fictional character is known as the "boy who wouldn't grow up"?

A. Peter Pan, from a 1904 play by James M. Barrie called *Peter Pan, the Boy Who Wouldn't Grow Up*

Q. What type of dragon did Viktor Krum face in book four of the Harry Potter series?

A. a Chinese Fireball (in *Harry Potter and the Goblet of Fire* by J. K. Rowling)

Q. Can you name all the dwarfs in the movie *Snow White and the Seven Dwarfs?*

A. Bashful, Doc, Dopey, Grumpy, Happy, Sleepy, and Sneezy

Q. Street names from a real place were used in the original version of the Monopoly board game. What is the city?

A. Atlantic City, New Jersey

Q. In *The Wizard of Oz*, who wanted Dorothy's shoes?

A. the Wicked Witch of the West

Q. Match the superhero with his secret identity:

1. Barry Allen, police scientist
2. Bruce Banner, scientist
3. Hal Jordan, test pilot
4. Matt Murdock, lawyer

    a. Daredevil

    b. The Flash

    c. The Green Lantern

    d. The Incredible Hulk

A. 1-b; 2-d; 3-c; 4-a

Q. In the Harry Potter books, what is the animal shop in Diagon Alley called?

A. Magical Menagerie

Science Fair

It takes a space probe about 7 to 10 months to get to Mars.

In 1962, U.S. astronaut John Glenn became the first American to eat in space. He ate applesauce squeezed from a tube. (Glenn's meal helped scientists learn how humans were affected by weightlessness in space.)

The Holland Tunnel was the world's first long, mechanically ventilated underwater tunnel for motor vehicles. Opened in 1927, it connects New York and New Jersey under the Hudson River, and it is still in use.

A scanning tunneling microscope is powerful enough to bring the structure of an atom into focus!

The Beaufort scale is used to measure the speed of wind. It was named for the man who devised it, Sir Francis Beaufort (pronounced *BOH-furt*).

Scientists studying the DNA of a 9,000-year-old skeleton found in England discovered that the skeleton had a living descendant—a local schoolteacher!

A *paleontologist* is a scientist who studies fossils.

If you could drive from Earth to the sun at a speed of 60 miles per hour, it would take about 177 years to get there.

Famous Folks

John D. Rockefeller built the first modern industrial empire. Through his Standard Oil Company, Rockefeller controlled nearly all of the production, processing, and marketing of oil in the U.S.

Vincent van Gogh (1853–1890) created more than 800 oil paintings and 700 drawings. Today, one of his paintings may sell for millions of dollars. During his lifetime, however, he was poverty stricken and sold only one painting.

Samuel Langhorne Clemens was the real name of Mark Twain, creator of Tom Sawyer and Huckleberry Finn. Clemens took his pen name from a riverboat term, *mark twain*, which means "two fathoms deep" (a depth of about 12 feet).

In 1879, Belva Ann Lockwood became the first woman to argue a case before the U.S. Supreme Court.

Alexander Graham Bell's mother and wife were both unable to use his famous invention, the telephone. They were deaf.

A frontierswoman who was born Martha Jane Cannary was buried in South Dakota with a gun in each hand. She also was known by her married name, Martha Jane Burke. However, she was much more famous by another name: Calamity Jane.

The Boston Tea Party of 1773, one of the most famous protests in American history, was organized by Samuel Adams. (He was second cousin to John Adams, a founding father and the second president of the U.S.)

ANYONE HUNGRY?

A pineapple is a fruit that starts out as lavender-colored flowers. The flowers fuse, developing into the pineapple fruit.

The chemical in chili peppers that makes them hot is called capsaicin.

Garlic belongs to the lily family of plants (Liliaceae).

About 60 percent of all sandwiches eaten in the U.S. are hamburgers.

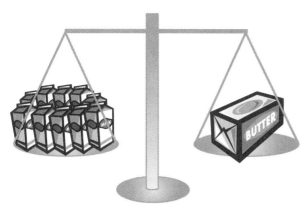

About 10 quarts of milk are needed to make one pound of butter.

About 30,000 peanut-butter sandwiches can be made from one acre of peanuts.

About 70 percent of all the popcorn consumed in the U.S. is eaten in the home.

Potato chips were originally called Saratoga chips.

Americans eat more than 100 acres of pizza each day.

WAY BACK WHEN

Christopher Columbus made four expeditions to the New World.

In ancient Greece, one of the most popular male fashions was wearing a beard—fake beards as well as real ones.

Giving Easter eggs to children grew out of the tradition of giving eggs to friends in the spring, which began in ancient Persia (now Iran).

On September 22, 1776, just before being hanged as a spy, 21-year-old Nathan Hale spoke these now-famous words: "I only regret that I have but one life to lose for my country." Hale, a schoolteacher, had joined the American army during the American Revolution.

The first hard candies, produced to relieve coughing, were made in Egypt, around 1000 B.C.

An early form of the bicycle, first seen in the 18th century, was known as a "dandy horse."

At one point in history, people in Scotland refused to eat potatoes, because they were not mentioned in the Bible.

The coffee plant originated in what today is Ethiopia. Using the beans to make a drink began in Arabia in the 15th century.

According to legend, twins named Romulus and Remus founded the city of Rome, Italy. As babies, they were swept down the Tiber River, but landed safely. A wolf and a woodpecker took care of them until a herdsman found them.

ANIMAL ANTICS

Q. Are all lobsters red?

A. Only those that have been cooked in hot water. In nature, lobsters are many colors, including blue, gray, greenish-brown, and yellow—but never red.

Q. What is a Gila monster?

A. a type of lizard (pronounced HEE-luh) It is one of only two lizard species that are poisonous. The other is the Mexican beaded lizard

Q. At what age does a filly become a mare?

A. four years

Q. What is a group of kangaroos called?

A. a troop (other collective nouns for kangaroos: "herd" and "mob")

Q. In which direction does a fly take off from a horizontal surface?

A. upward and backward (Now you know which way to aim the flyswatter!)

$

Q. What type of whale has a head that is 20 feet long, 10 feet high, and 7 feet wide?

A. the sperm whale

Q. How many living species of bears are there?

A. eight: the Asiatic black bear, the American black bear, the brown bear, the giant panda, the polar bear, the sloth bear, the spectacled bear, and the sun bear

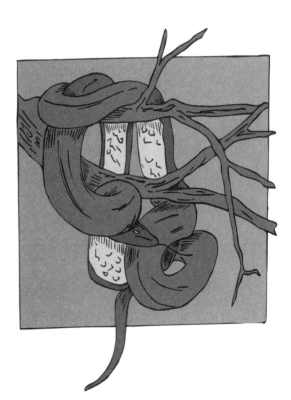

Q. What type of snake weighs more than any other?

A. the anaconda (It can weigh more than 1,100 pounds.)

Q. How many different species of penguins are there?

A. 17

151

Horseshoes, a common symbol of good luck, are always hung with the open end pointed upward—so that the good luck will not drain out.

The world's largest collection of baseball cards is not at the National Baseball Hall of Fame, but at the Metropolitan Museum of Art in New York City. The museum has thousands of cards in its collection, too many to show at once. A rotating exhibit shows different cards, 16 sets at a time.

Before making a fortune in computer games, Nintendo manufactured playing cards.

In Japan, most cars are sold by door-to-door salespersons who visit the homes of potential customers.

The "black boxes" that record flight data on commercial airplanes are not black. They are orange.

To get one ounce of royal-purple dye for Cleopatra's clothes, 20,000 snails had to be soaked for 10 days.

AUGUST						
1	2	3	4	5	6	7
8	9	10	11	12	13	14
15	16	17	18	19	20	21
22	23	24	25	26	27	28
29	30	31				

A Friday the 13th will occur in any month in which the first day is a Sunday.

Rubber toy balloons were introduced in 1825. Before then, they were made of animal bladders or intestines filled with water or air.

Where in the World?

China has more land frontiers than any other country. It borders 14 independent countries: Afghanistan, Bhutan, India, Kazakhstan, Kyrgyzstan, Laos, Mongolia, Myanmar (Burma), Nepal, North Korea, Pakistan, Russia, Tajikistan, and Vietnam.

The Caspian Sea is the largest inland body of water in the world. It lies in Central Asia, and covers 149,200 square miles of land—an area larger than Germany.

Not counting the continent of Australia, Greenland is the largest island on Earth.

Of the world's 193 independent countries, only two have a name that begins with *A* but does not end with *A*: Afghanistan and Azerbaijan. (Other *A*-starting countries are Albania, Algeria, Andorra, Angola, Antigua, Argentina, Armenia, Australia, and Austria.)

The city of Venice, Italy, is made up of 118 small islands, connected by about 150 canals and 400 bridges.

ALASKA

MOVE OVER, THERE IS ROOM FOR 21 OF US!

The smallest 21 U.S. states would fit into the land area of Alaska.

The Canary Islands were not named after birds. The name is from *canes (KAH-nez)*, the Latin word for "dogs."

The longest suspension bridge in the world is Akashi Kaikyo Bridge in Japan. It has a main span of 6,570 feet. (That is 1.24 miles!)

IT'S SOME BODY!

HMMM . . . WHERE IS IT?

The smallest bone in your body is the stapes *(STAY-peez)*, also called the stirrup. It is in your ear.

If you could spread out the surface of the inside of your lungs, it would be the size of a tennis court.

The skin of an adult human weighs five to eight pounds.

At rest, an adult's heart beats about 72 times per minute. That is 4,320 beats an hour—103,680 beats a day—and more than 37 million beats in a year!

There are 26 bones in each human foot. This means that about one-quarter of all the bones in your body are in your feet! There are even more in your hands— 27 bones each.

Like fingerprints, every person's tongue print is unique.

Arteries and veins are both blood vessels. So what is the difference? *Arteries* carry oxygen-rich blood *from* the heart through the body. *Veins* carry the depleted blood *to* the heart for more oxygen.

In the U.S., the average person eats about 17 pounds of cereal per year.

The human mouth produces one-quarter to one-half gallon of saliva each day.

Nature Notes

The rings around the planet Saturn are composed of chunks of rock and ice.

Two elements, together, comprise 98 percent of all known matter in the universe: hydrogen (about 73 percent) and helium (about 25 percent).

There are about 1,650 different species of cactus plants.

Lightning strikes Earth about 8.6 million times a day.

Most tornadoes on Earth occur in the central/southeastern U.S.

The greatest known deposit of copper in the world is in Chile, in the Andes Mountains.

Pecans come from hickory trees. The pecan tree is one of several species of hickory. Hickory trees belong to the same family as walnuts, but the nuts of the two trees are quite different.

Old Faithful, in Yellowstone National Park, is the most famous geyser in North America.

A *supernova* is the explosion of a very large, collapsing star.

The Amazing U.S.A.

The U.S. Congress officially recognized "Uncle Sam" as a national symbol in 1961. The term *Uncle Sam* as a nickname for the United States has been around a long time. It was first used during the War of 1812.

Petrified wood is the official state gem of Washington.

Jousting has been the official sport of Maryland since 1962.

Have you ever noticed the two Latin mottoes on the back of a U.S. dollar bill? *ANNUIT CŒPTIS* means "He [God] has favored our undertakings." *NOVUS ORDO SECLORUM* means "A new order of the ages."

"Little red schoolhouses" were painted red because red paint was the cheapest available.

The Smithsonian Institution in Washington, D.C., was founded as a gift from James Smithson—an English scientist who had never set foot in the U.S.!

The Great Seal of the United States was officially adopted by the Continental Congress in 1782. The Great Seal is still used today. Over the centuries, only minor changes have been made to the original design.

More American soldiers lost their lives during the Civil War than in any other war in which U.S. troops have fought. More than 617,500 soldiers were killed—about 359,500 from the North and about 258,000 from the South.

The state with the largest proven crude-oil reserves is Texas (nearly five million barrels).

SPORTS STUFF

Q. How many consecutive strikes does it take to bowl a perfect game?

A. 12 (a score of 300)

Q. Which kind of sporting equipment outsells baseballs, basketballs, and footballs combined?

A. Frisbees

Q. In rodeo-competition bull riding, how long must the rider hang on?

A. eight seconds

Q. Cy Young holds the record for most games won by a major-league pitcher: 511. What was his real name?

A. Denton True Young (Cy was short for "cyclone," because of the speed of his fastball.)

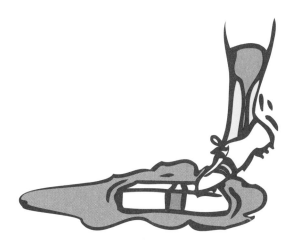

Q. What game requires t... playing field?

A. ...olo (Those ponies need a lot of ...m to run! A polo field is 300 ...s long and 160 yards wide.)

Q. In baseball, the distance between bases is 90 feet. What is the size of first, second, and third bases?

A. 15" × 15" (and 3" deep)

Q. A feathery was an item used in which sport in the 17th century?

A. golf (A feathery was a golf ball made from boiled feathers that were squeezed into a stitched-leather cover.)

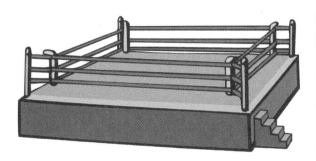

Q. Which heavyweight boxing champ was once knocked out of the ring in the first round, yet came back to win in the second round?

A. Jack Dempsey (against Luis Angel Firpo on September 14, 1923)

Q. Who was the only pro basketball player to score 100 points in a single regulation game?

A. Wilt Chamberlain on March 2, 1962, vs. the New York Knicks (Chamberlain's Philadelphia Warriors won, 169–147.)

ANIMAL ANTICS

The tiny red-billed quelea, which is native to East Africa, has the greatest population of any living bird. More than four million can live in an area smaller than 125 acres.

The call of the world's loudest insect, the African cicada, can be as loud as 106.7 decibels—about the same loudness as a car horn.

Although the wolf spider looks pretty nasty, its bite is not harmful to humans.

The emu, the kiwi, the ostrich, and the penguin are all birds that cannot fly.

A cat has a better memory than a dog.

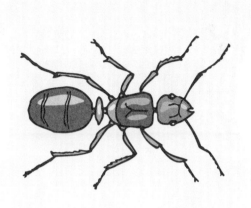

The animal with the largest brain in proportion to its size is the ant.

The bumblebee bat, weighing less than a penny, is the smallest mammal in the world.

A baby blue whale can drink about 44 gallons of milk a day and gain 7 pounds an hour!

A camel is fully mature at six to eight years of age.

TV, Movies, Music, & More

Gene Autry was a famous "singing cowboy" of movies and one-time owner of the Texas Rangers baseball team. He has another claim to fame: In 1948, he recorded "Rudolph the Red-nosed Reindeer," a song that remains an all-time hit.

The planet in *The Planet of the Apes*, a popular sci-fi book, was Earth. (The book, by Pierre Boulle, was the basis of several movies.)

The final episode of the series *M*A*S*H* holds the record for largest audience rating in TV history. More than 105.4 million viewers in 50.15 million homes—about 77 percent of all viewers—tuned in to watch that program on February 28, 1983.

The first thing that Clark Kent takes off when changing into Superman is his eyeglasses.

Early prints of the 1931 film *Frankenstein* had some scenes tinted green, the "color of fear." Audiences found them so horrible that they were pulled from theaters and replaced by prints that were all black and white.

In *The Lord of the Rings*, Gollum's real name is Smeagol.

There are 100 letter tiles in a Scrabble crossword game.

The Adventures of Tom Sawyer, by Mark Twain, was the first manuscript produced on a typewriter.

Film star Charlie Chaplin once lost a Charlie Chaplin look-alike contest.

Science Fair

A *hygrometer* is an instrument that measures the relative humidity of air. You don't need special equipment, though—human hair is a natural hygrometer. Hair tends to curl as moisture in the air increases, and to straighten in dry conditions.

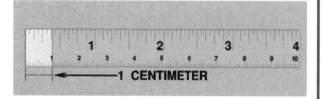

1 CENTIMETER

Most countries today use the *metric* system of measurement, which includes meters for distance and liters for volume. The U.S. uses a different system, which includes miles, yards, and feet for distance, and quarts and gallons for volume. It is known as the *imperial* system.

In 1839, Thedor Schwann, a German biologist, published *Microscopic Researches Into Accordance in the Structure and Growth of Animals and Plants.* Schwann's careful studies of plant and animal life helped convince other scientists of an idea that we now take for granted—that cells are the basic unit of all animal life.

In 1997, researchers in Scotland performed the first successful cloning of an adult mammal. A lamb known as Dolly was created from a single cell taken from a sheep. The lamb was an exact genetic copy of the sheep.

A *pathologist* is a scientist who studies diseases—their causes, how they develop and progress, and their effects on the body. Some pathologists specialize in problems other than disease. For instance, a *speech pathologist* studies stuttering and other speech problems. A *forensic pathologist* looks for a cause of death.

Karl Benz, a German engineer, built the first automobile powered by an internal-combustion engine. His three-wheel vehicle had its first successful test drive in 1885.

Halley's Comet

In 1705, astronomer Edmond Halley said that large comets seen in 1531, 1607, and 1682 were all the *same* comet—and that it would return in 1758. It did! Records of the comet's visits go back as far as 240 B.C. Its last visit was in 1985–1986. It next will be visible from Earth in 2061.

"Good to the last drop," a phrase that is still used in ads for a brand of coffee, was coined by President Theodore Roosevelt.

Franklin D. Roosevelt was the only person elected president four times, and he served longer than any other U.S. president (1933–1945). That won't happen again. In 1955, the Constitution was changed, limiting presidents to two terms.

Four Score and seven years ago...

The phrase "of the people, by the people, and for the people" is from the Gettysburg Address, a speech made by President Abraham Lincoln on November 19, 1863.

When George Washington was president, slaves made up 20 percent of the U.S. population. At the time, however, census takers counted each slave as three fifths of a person.

Woodrow Wilson was the first U.S. president to visit Europe while in office. He went there in December 1918 to take part in the Paris Peace Conference.

Richard M. Nixon was the first U.S. president to place a telephone call to the moon. On July 20, 1969, he spoke with astronauts Neil Armstrong and Edwin "Buzz" Aldrin—the first people to set foot on Earth's closest neighbor.

Eleven-year-old Grace Bedell wrote a letter to Abraham Lincoln, suggesting that he would get more votes if he grew a beard.

President Thomas Jefferson is credited with introducing waffles and macaroni to the U.S. He found out how to make macaroni while touring Italy, and took a waffle iron home to Virginia after tasting waffles in the Netherlands.

171

THIS and THAT

Q. What was the first automobile mass-produced in the U.S.?

A. The Oldsmobile, manufactured by Ransome Eli Olds in 1901. (About 12 years later, Henry Ford invented an improved assembly-line process.)

Q. What is the main use, by humans, of squirrel hairs?

A. They are used to make camel-hair paintbrushes. The brushes are also made with goat, pony, and ox hair, but not with hair from camels.

Q. What is the most common surname in the world?

A. Chang

Q. What company was the first to mass-market rubber-soled shoes as canvas-topped sneakers?

A. Keds, in 1917

172

Q. Where does the saying "Don't count your chickens before they are hatched" come from?

A. an Aesop's fable

Q. During what century is Robin Hood said to have robbed from the rich and given to the poor?

A. the 12th century

Q. How many dollar bills, laid lengthwise end to end, would it take to encircle Earth at the equator?

A. 256,964,529 dollar bills (Earth's circumference at equator: 24,901.55 miles; a dollar bill's length: 6.14 inches)

Q. Whose heart beats faster: an adult human's or an elephant's?

A. an adult human's (adult human's heart: 70 to 80 beats per minute; elephant's heart: about 25 beats per minute)

WHAT'S THE WORD?

The saying "Love makes the world go round" comes from the Middle Ages. According to religious teachings of that time, love was what set the universe in motion.

The Chinese characters for the word *gunpowder* translate as "fire medicine."

The first person to use the word *nerd* was Dr. Seuss, in his 1950 book *If I Ran the Zoo.*

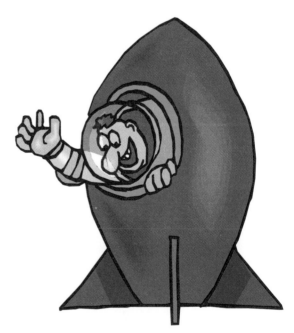

The word *good-bye* is a contraction of the phrase "God be with you" or "Good be with you."

The average American 14-year-old has a vocabulary of about 10,000 words. (In 1950, it was 25,000 words.)

Leathernecks is a nickname for the U.S. Marines. It comes from the high leather collars, called stocks, that were part of the early uniform of British marines. (Stocks were designed to force marines to keep their chins up.)

A E I O U
H K L M N P W

The Hawaiian alphabet has only 12 letters—5 vowels and 7 consonants.

Hoosegow is a slang term meaning "jail." It comes from *juzgado*, a Mexican-Spanish word that means "judge."

Famous Folks

In 1930, Sinclair Lewis became the first American to win the Nobel Prize for Literature. He wrote a number of famous novels, including *Main Street*, *Babbitt*, *Arrowsmith*, and *Dodsworth*.

In 1849, Elizabeth Blackwell became the first woman to graduate from a U.S. medical school (ranking first in her class), and the first female doctor of medicine.

One of the many sayings that Benjamin Franklin wrote for his *Poor Richard's Almanack* of 1733 was this: "The heart of a fool is in his mouth, but the mouth of a wise man is in his heart."

U.S. naval hero John Paul Jones was only 21 when he became captain of his own ship.

During World War II, Princess Elizabeth (now queen of England) wanted to contribute to the war effort. She did so by repairing military vehicles.

Henry Wadsworth Longfellow, who wrote *The Song of Hiawatha* and other famous poems, was one of the first people in the U.S. to have indoor plumbing.

Journalist Nellie Bly is famous for her record-setting around-the-world trip, which she accomplished in 72 days, 6 hours, 11 minutes, and 14 seconds in 1889.

Harry Houdini, considered America's greatest magician and illusionist, claimed that he was born in Appleton, Wisconsin. He did grow up there, but his real birthplace was Budapest, Hungary.

ANIMAL ANTICS

Celestial, comet, and lionhead are all breeds of goldfish.

To keep out sand, the camel has three eyelids per eye. One of the three eyelids is very thin. The other two have long, thick eyelashes. A camel also can close its nostrils.

Most calico cats are female. Only one out of every 3,000 calicos born is a male.

A caterpillar's head has six eyes on each side. That is 12 total!

The giraffe and the okapi are the only two animals in the family Giraffidae. Both live in Africa—okapis in the central rain forests, giraffes in open grassland areas.

An ant can lift more than 20 times its own weight, and pull about 50 times its own weight.

A donkey has no trouble seeing where it is going. The position of its eyes allows it to see all four feet at the same time.

A hedgehog's heart beats 190 times per minute. That is about two and a half times as fast as yours.

You can tell the age of a mountain goat by counting the rings on its horns. The first ring develops about age two; another is added each spring.

Science Fair

Edwin Land, the inventor of Polaroid "instant" cameras, also invented polarized lenses, which prevent glare, for sunglasses.

In 1893, Whitcomb Judson was granted a patent for an invention that he called a "clasp locker"— the zipper.

Explorer I was the first successful man-made satellite launched by the U.S. It was launched on January 31, 1958—four months after the world's first successful satellite, *Sputnik*, was launched by the Soviet Union.

Garrett Augustus Morgan invented two life-saving devices: the gas mask (1916) and the traffic light (patented 1923).

The first practical lawn mower was invented in 1830.

A telescope on top of Mauna Kea in Hawaii is so powerful that it can see a penny-sized object more than five miles away!

A *nematologist* (nem-uh-TAHL-uh-jist) is a scientist who studies roundworms.

Dust from outer space—from meteors and other space bodies—falls to Earth, causing Earth's weight to increase by about 90 tons per day.

A *botanist* is a scientist who studies plants.

181

Nature Notes

Q. Which animal flies highest, the geoduck or the shelduck?

A. That is a trick question! The shelduck is a small member of the duck family. Like other ducks, it can fly. The geoduck, however, is a large member of the clam family. It can weigh up to eight pounds.

Q. The moon has no atmosphere. Does that make it warmer or colder than Earth?

A. Both. The side facing the sun gets very hot—about 250 degrees Fahrenheit. Without a "blanket" of atmosphere to hold in some of that heat, the temperature on the side facing away from the sun drops to -290 degrees Fahrenheit.

Q. When does a snowstorm become a blizzard?

A. When wind speed reaches at least 35 miles per hour, the temperature drops below 20 degrees Fahrenheit, and visibility is less than one-quarter of a mile.

Q. What does it mean when someone calls a tree *deciduous* (*dih-SIH-juh-wus*)?

A. *Deciduous* trees shed all their leaves one season a year, then grow them back another. Maples and oaks are examples of deciduous trees. *Evergreen* trees, such as pines, have green leaves (needles) year-round.

182

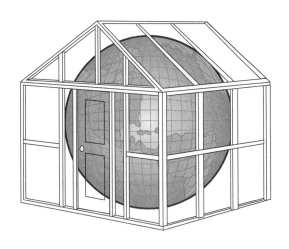

Q. What is the greenhouse effect?

A. when sunlight passes through Earth's atmosphere and its heat is trapped close to Earth's surface, raising the temperature

Q. What is the difference between a nature reserve and a national park?

A. Both are areas that have been set aside for the protection of the animals and/or plants that live there. However, national parks are open to the public, for people to visit and enjoy, while nature reserves are for wildlife only.

Q. What type of flower is the world's smallest?

A. the *Lemna*, also known as duck-weed, and the *Wolffia*, also known as watermeal (These tiny plants float on the surface of still water. The blossom is smaller than the head of a pin. The entire plant is only 1/16 inch to 1/8 inch across.)

Q. What type of flower is the world's largest?

A. *Rafflesia arnoldii*, also known as the monster flower, which grows in Malaysia (Its bloom can be a yard across and weigh 24 pounds. It also is the world's stinkiest flower. Its rotting-meat smell attracts flies the way sweet-scented flowers attract bees.)

THIS and THAT

In China, a bride wears red on her wedding day.

In most displays and advertisements, the hands of a clock or watch are set at 10:10.

Since 1872, the official colors of Mardi Gras in New Orleans, Louisiana, have been purple, gold, and green.

The largest cathedral in the world is the Cathedral Church of St. John the Divine in New York, New York.

Pierre Lorillard IV invented a now-familiar type of formal clothing for the Autumn Ball of 1886. It was called a tuxedo—named for Tuxedo Park, New York, where the formal dance took place.

The Pluto Platter was the original name of Walter Frederick Morrison's invention, the Frisbee.

In 1897, Americans' average life span was 48 years. It rose to 65 years by 1947, and to 76.1 years by 1997. Experts think that it will reach 100 years or more by 2027.

The first auto manufacturer to offer seat belts was Nash, in 1950. They were an optional feature.

The Silver Buffalo Award is the highest honor given by the Boy Scouts of America.

ANIMAL ANTICS

Every day, a ruby-throated hummingbird must eat 100 percent of its body weight.

The average hen lays about five eggs per week.

The earliest ancestor of the horse was about the size of a modern-day fox. It was called *Eohippus,* or dawn horse.

Bees and wasps are responsible for more human deaths each year than poisonous snakes are.

Of the roughly 4,660 groups of mammals, the largest is rodents. There are more than 2,050 known living species of them.

About 99.9 percent of all animal species that ever lived on Earth were extinct by the time humans first appeared.

The breed of dog most commonly used in search-and-rescue operations is the German shepherd.

The basking shark is the second-largest fish in the ocean. It can be up to 46 feet long. (The whale shark is the largest.)

The giant panda is an endangered species. Fewer than 1,000 are left in the wild, mostly in China. Another 100 or so live in zoos around the world.

SPORTS STUFF

Nolan Ryan pitched more no-hitters and struck out more batters than any other pitcher in major-league baseball. In his 27-season career, Ryan pitched 7 no-hit games and struck out 5,714 batters.

The Little League was formed in 1939. At the time, it was for boys only.

No horse has ever won the Kentucky Derby two times—because the race is for three-year-old horses only.

Kareem Abdul-Jabbar scored the most career points in NBA basketball history: 38,387.

The very first Olympic Games, held in Greece in 776 B.C., consisted of only one event: a 210-yard race.

The same team won the first four championships of the WNBA—Women's National Basketball Association. From 1997, when the WNBA started, through 2000, the Houston Comets were the queens of the b-ball court!

In 1975, Frank Robinson became the first African-American manager of a major-league baseball team—the Cleveland Indians.

The world's largest bowling center is in Japan.

The first televised basketball game was played at Madison Square Garden, in New York City, on February 28, 1940.

Science Fair

Q. What is tetrafluoroethylene resin?

A. The substance better known as Teflon. A chemist named Roy J. Plunkett discovered it in 1939. Teflon has an unusual property: One side clings fast to another surface (such as a metal cooking pan). Few things, however, will stick to its other side.

Q. What do dynamite and the Nobel Peace Prize have in common?

A. A man named Alfred Bernhard Nobel. Nobel invented dynamite in 1867. Nobel died in 1896. In his will, he left instructions for the establishment of prizes to honor great humanitarian, scientific, and literary achievements.

Q. What is *syzygy (SIH-zuh-jee)*?

A. *Syzygy* is when three bodies in the solar system—such as Earth, the moon, and the sun—lie in or close to a straight line. This happens twice a month, when the moon is new (its dark side faces Earth) and when it is full (completely lit).

Q. How fast does sound travel?

A. The speed of sound varies, depending on the altitude and on the temperature and density of the air it is traveling through. At sea level the speed of sound is about 761 miles per hour.

Q. What is Sedna?

A. a planetlike object orbiting the sun, discovered in 2003. Sedna is the most distant known object in the solar system. Sedna is so far out that it takes 10,500 Earth years for it to orbit the sun.

Q. Which star in our Milky Way galaxy is closest to Earth?

A. the sun. It is 92,980,000 miles away. Its light, which travels at 186,000 miles per second, takes 8.3 minutes to reach Earth.

Q. What does it mean when a weather forecaster says, "It will be partly cloudy"?

A. It means that clouds will block out 35 to 65 percent of the sky. "Mostly clear" or "mostly sunny" means that only 12 to 25 percent is blocked, while "mostly cloudy" is 75 to 90 percent and "cloudy" is 90 to 100 percent blocked.

Q. What does a physicist study?

A. Physicists are scientists who study matter and energy: what they are made of, and how they behave and interact.

WAY BACK WHEN

Glass was first made in ancient Egypt, around 3500 B.C.

The world's first successful oil well was drilled in Pennsylvania in 1859.

Susan B. Anthony was the first woman to appear on U.S. currency. Her portrait is on one-dollar coins issued by the U.S. Mint in 1979.

The first shot of the American Revolution—known as "the shot heard 'round the world"—was fired at Lexington, Massachusetts, on April 19, 1775.

The Empire State Building's official opening was in 1931. Once the world's tallest building, it was designed by Shreve, Lamb, and Harmon, an architectural company.

DINERS CLUB
INTERNATIONAL

Jane Q. Public

1200 35697722 3689   03/08

The first credit card was issued in 1950, by a company called Diner's Club.

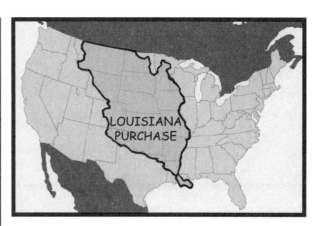

When President Thomas Jefferson bought the Louisiana Territory from France in 1803, the price was two cents per acre—a total cost of $15 million.

The first religious group to oppose slavery in America was the Quakers, also known as the Society of Friends.

The first shopping mall, the Country Club Plaza, was founded in 1922 by the J. C. Nichols company, in Kansas City, Missouri.

TV, Movies, Music, & More

MOVIES

The first movie to win an Academy Award® for best picture was *Wings*, in 1929.

The TV interview program *Meet the Press* is the longest-running show on network television. It premiered on November 6, 1947.

Lego started producing its toy building blocks in 1949. The blocks were called Automatic Binding Bricks.

The record for the most number-one hit singles in the U.S. is held by the Beatles, who have 20. In second place is Elvis Presley, with 18.

Sherlock Holmes, the world-famous fictional detective, lives at 221B Baker Street in London, England.

The dog owned by the Grinch in *How the Grinch Stole Christmas* is named Max.

Barbra Streisand was the first performer to win an Oscar®, Emmy®, Tony®, and Grammy® award.

In 1955, *The Wizard of Oz* became the first Hollywood movie to be shown on TV.

Bela Lugosi, famous for playing Count Dracula in the movies, was buried as he requested—wearing Dracula's long black cape.

ANIMAL ANTICS

Yummy

Butterflies "taste" with their feet. Sense organs in their feet detect sweetness, letting them know if they have landed on a plant with nectar they will like.

The basenji is known as "the barkless dog." It can't bark—but it does make yodeling sounds. This short-haired hunting dog—a type of hound— was originally bred in central Africa.

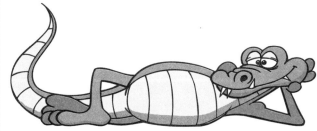

Crocodiles don't spend so much time lying on riverbanks because they are lazy. Like other reptiles, crocs are cold-blooded. They get warm by lying in the sun, and those big bodies take time to heat up. Growing up to 20 feet long and 1,000 pounds, crocs are the largest and heaviest living reptiles.

Cats have powerful backs, shoulders, and legs. A cat's backbone is supported by strong muscles, and this gives the animal great strength and flexibility—perfect for leaping, pouncing, and stretching.

Smokey the Bear—a black bear cub rescued from a 1950 forest fire—may have been the most popular bear ever. How popular? Smokey got so much mail that, in 1964, the U.S. Postal Service gave him his own ZIP code!

Bats are not really blind. They see best in the dark, but they cannot see color.

Temnodontosaurus platyodon had the largest eye of any animal: 10.4 inches across. That is about as wide as an adult human head is long! The fishlike sea reptile lived before the time of the dinosaurs. The only animal now living that comes close to that record is the giant squid. Its eye is estimated to be 10 inches across.

IT'S SOME BODY!

The human heart, which is about the size of a fist, weighs an average 9 ounces in females and 10.5 in males.

Toenails grow about a half to a third more slowly than fingernails.

You blink your eyes about 4.2 million times a year.

In moderate conditions, an adult will sweat about 0.37 quart of fluid. Working or exercising in hot or humid conditions, the same person can lose up to 2 quarts!

It is impossible to
lick your elbow.

The average American adult
eats about 1 ton of food a
year. That is about 77 tons in
a lifetime—roughly the weight
of 9.6 elephants!

Each taste bud on your tongue
is made up of 50 to 75 taste-
receptor cells. These special cells
die out and are replaced by new
ones every seven to ten days.

There are 270 bones in your
body at birth. By the time you
are grown up, however, you
have only 206. As you grow,
many of the smaller bones join
together to form larger ones.

PRESIDENTS ON PARADE

Q. Eight U.S. presidents were born in Virginia—more than in any other state. What state was the birthplace of seven presidents?

A. Ohio.

Q. Who was the only U.S. president elected to two nonconsecutive terms in office?

A. Grover Cleveland (Counted as the 22nd and 24th president, he served 1885–1889 and 1893–1897.)

Q. What do presidents Grover Cleveland, Abraham Lincoln, Harry S. Truman, and George Washington have in common?

A. They never attended college.

Q. Until 1980, when Ronald Reagan was elected president at age 69, who was the oldest person elected to that office?

A. William Henry Harrison, who was 67 when elected in 1840

Q. Which U.S. president has the most places named after him?

A. George Washington (257 townships, 121 cities and towns, 33 counties, and 1 state)

Q. Who were the first residents of the White House?

A. President John Adams and his wife, Abigail Adams

Q. Who was Abraham Lincoln's running mate when he ran for president in 1860?

A. Hannibal Hamlin

Q. President Ronald Reagan loved jelly beans. During his eight years in office, about how much of the candy did the White House buy?

A. about 12 tons

Q. Who is buried in Grant's tomb?

A. Technically, no one. President Ulysses S. Grant and his wife, Julia Dent Grant, are entombed there, in stone coffins in an aboveground chamber. *Buried* means put in a hole in the ground and covered with earth.

SPORTS STUFF

Rowing is the oldest college sport still played at U.S. colleges.

Satchel Paige is the only pitcher to enter the National Baseball Hall of Fame with a losing major-league record. That is because Paige spent most of his stellar professional career in the Negro Leagues, before blacks were allowed to play in the major leagues.

On April 8, 1974, Hank Aaron of the Atlanta Braves hit his 715th home run, breaking Babe Ruth's record of 714. The pitcher who served up Aaron's mighty blast was Al Downing of the Los Angeles Dodgers.

A karate training hall is called a dojo.

The oldest organized sport in the U.S. is horse racing. The first official race was run on Long Island, New York, in 1665.

Bill Russell was the first African-American to coach a major professional sports team in the U.S. He became coach of the NBA's Boston Celtics in 1966.

The last major-league baseball team to put up lights for night games was the Chicago Cubs. The first full night game played at the Cubs' Wrigley Field took place on August 9, 1988. (They started a game there on August 8, but it was rained out after three and a half innings.)

The first athlete to ever win seven gold medals at one Olympics was American swimmer Mark Spitz, in 1972. With the two golds that he won in 1968, Spitz earned a grand total of nine Olympic gold medals!

The Vezina Trophy is an award given each year to the top goalie in the NHL.

ANIMAL ANTICS

The anableps is also known as the four-eyed fish. It really has only two eyes, but each eye is divided into two parts. Lying with half of each eye above the water and half below, the anableps can watch for food in two places at once.

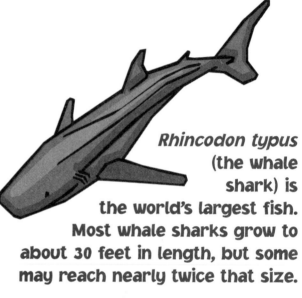

Rhincodon typus (the whale shark) is the world's largest fish. Most whale sharks grow to about 30 feet in length, but some may reach nearly twice that size.

Most starfish have five eyespots—one at the end of each arm. These eyes can't "see," but they can sense light.

The penguin is one of only a few birds that can swim but can't fly. (Others include the emu and the cassowary.)

Yawn! A giraffe sleeps only two to four hours a day.

A rat can fall from a five-story building without getting hurt.

How hungry are you? A ribbon worm will start eating itself if it can't find food.

The echidna, hedgehog, and porcupine are all mammals that have prickles.

Shrimp can swim backward.

WHAT'S THE WORD?

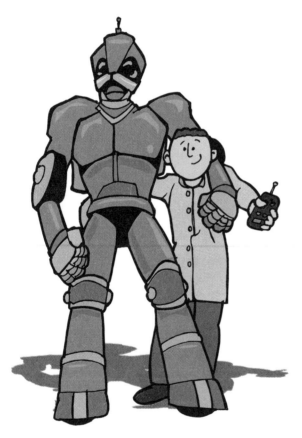

The word *robot* was coined by Karel Capek, a Czechoslovakian playwright. *Robot* comes from the Czech word *robota,* meaning "enforced labor." Capek used it in his 1921 play *R.U.R.* (short for "Rossum's Universal Robots").

The letters in the acronym laser stand for "**l**ight **a**mplification by **s**timulated **e**mission of **r**adiation." (An acronym is a word formed by the initial letters of words in a phrase.

Only four words in the English language end in *-dous:* *hazardous, horrendous, stupendous,* and *tremendous.*

For five years, *Webster's New International Dictionary* included an entry for a nonexistent word: *dord*.

Fido, a common name for a pet dog, comes from a Latin word meaning "faithful."

Have you ever seen *i.e.* or *e.g.* in a sentence? Both are abbreviations of Latin phrases. The *i.e.* stands for *id est*, meaning "it is." The *e.g.* stands for *exempli gratia*, which means "for the sake of example." We use it to say "for example."

What *do* female horses have to *do* with bad dreams? Nothing! The *mare* part of our word *nightmare* comes from the Old English word *maere*. A maere was an evil spirit said to attack people at night, while they slept.

Famous Folks

A woman—Queen Victoria of the United Kingdom—appeared on the first-ever postage stamp, issued in Britain in 1840. The first woman to appear on a U.S. postage stamp was Queen Isabella of Spain, in 1893.

It took Lewis and Clark 18 months to reach the Pacific Ocean on their historic trip, which began in St. Louis in 1804.

Napoleon Bonaparte, one of the most famous military leaders in history, was afraid of cats.

In 1501, at age 26, Michelangelo began sculpting his monumental statue *David*. He finished it in 1504.

Florence Nightingale, known as "the Lady of the Lamp," won fame for her nursing skills while caring for troops during the Crimean War (1854–1856).

Paul Revere is famous for his 1775 midnight ride, warning that the British were coming, but he wasn't a messenger by trade. He made his living as a silversmith.

Before Mohandas K. Gandhi—known as the Mahatma—became the leader of India's nonviolent independence movement, he earned his living as a lawyer.

Ludwig van Beethoven, the famous composer, poured ice water over his head when he sat down to create music. He believed that it stimulated his brain.

The Amazing U.S.A.

Q. Which U.S. war is associated with the slogan "Remember the *Maine*"?

A. the Spanish-American War of 1898 (The *Maine* was a U.S. battleship that was sunk in the harbor at Havana, Cuba, on February 15, 1898.)

Q. When did Native Americans officially become U.S. citizens?

A. in 1924, when the Indian Citizenship Act became law

Q. In what year was the first Easter egg roll held on the White House lawn?

A. 1878 (Before then, Easter egg rolls were held on the grounds of the U.S. Capitol.)

Q. What city was the first in the U.S. to establish a police department?

A. Boston, Massachusetts

Shawmut

Q. In 1630, John Winthrop changed the name of the Massachusetts settlement of Shawmut to what?

A. Boston

Q. On January 10, 1776, Thomas Paine published a pamphlet that became the battle cry for American independence. What was it called?

A. "Common Sense"

Q. What two Native American tribes are the only ones to have signed an official peace treaty with the U.S.?

A. the Miccosukee and the Seminole

Q. What is the only building to appear on two different U.S. notes of currency—the $2 bill and the $100 bill?

A. Independence Hall (The back of the $2 bill shows the signing of the Declaration of Independence, which took place inside the building. The back of the $100 bill shows the building's exterior.)

211

SPORTS STUFF

In slugger Babe Ruth's first professional baseball game—July 11, 1914—he was taken out for a pinch-hitter in the seventh inning!

The huddle in football got started when a deaf player, who communicated with his team members using sign language, wanted to keep the other team from seeing his hand signals.

On a regulation basketball court, the hoops are 10 feet high.

Until 1891, the baseball team now known as the Pittsburgh Pirates was called the Pittsburgh Innocents.

In 1970, only 127 people ran in the New York City marathon. In 2003, there were 34,729!

The longest overtime game in NHL playoff history was played in 1936. The Detroit Red Wings beat the Montreal Maroons in the sixth overtime period.

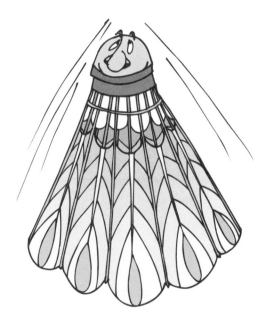

In Olympic badminton, the birdie or shuttlecock must have 16 feathers.

A "goofy-footed" skateboarder is one who is riding with the right foot forward.

Nature Notes

Diamonds may be black, pink, or yellow—or even blue, like the world-famous Hope diamond.

The coldest place in our solar system is Triton, one of Neptune's moons. It has a surface temperature of -391°F (-235°C).

A cool breeze coming off the ocean on a hot day is from warm air over land rising and cooler air over the water flowing in to replace it.

The most powerful earthquake ever recorded took place in Chile on May 22, 1960. It had a magnitude of 9.5 on the Richter scale.

The costliest hurricane (in terms of damage caused) ever to strike the U.S. was Hurricane Katrina, in 2005. It swept across parts of Louisiana, Alabama, and Mississippi, killing over 1800 people and causing damages of over $80 billion.

Aluminum is the most plentiful metallic element in Earth's crust.

Pepper plants grown in hotter temperatures yield the hottest peppers, but too much direct sunlight can harm the plant.

It takes the nectar from about two million flowers for honeybees to produce one pound of honey.

You might see dew or frost without fog, but you will never see fog without dew or frost.

215

ANIMAL ANTICS

The collie breed was developed as a working dog in Scotland during the 17th century.

The rhinoceros beetle may be the strongest animal in proportion to its size. It can support up to 850 times its own weight.

India has more cattle than any other country—more than 300 million.

A single beaver can cut down about 200 trees in a year.

A prairie dog is not a dog. It is a rodent.

The goby is the world's smallest fish. The smallest type of goby, *Pandaka pygmaea*, is only three-eighths of an inch long.

The first U.S. endangered-species list was issued in 1967. Seventy-seven animals appeared on that first list, including the American alligator, the California condor, and the Colorado River squawfish.

When a penguin is cold, it turns its back to the sun. The black feathers on its back absorb heat from the sun. The white feathers on its front reflect the heat.

Cats have about 100 vocal sounds.

Science Fair

Q. How fast does a lightning bolt travel?

A. about 60,000 miles per second

Q. What did Johann Wilhelm Ritter discover in 1801?

A. ultraviolet light—part of the color spectrum of light that is invisible to the human eye

Q. Who was Peking man?

A. An early ancestor of humans. Our knowledge of him is based on fossilized bones, 130,000 to 900,000 years old, that were found in China near Beijing (once known as Peking). Peking man had a thick skull and brow, with a small forehead and large jaw.

Q. What country uses more industrial robots than any other?

A. Japan (It uses more than half of the world total.)

Q. Who invented the electric battery?

A. Alessandro Volta (1745–1827), an Italian physicist

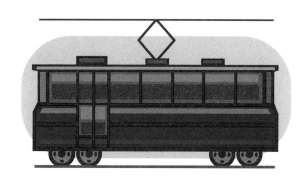

Q. The first public electric railway opened in 1881. Where?

A. In Germany. It was an electric tramway that ran from Lichterfelde, near Berlin, to a cadet academy—a distance of about 1.7 miles.

Q. Who was the first person to use a parachute—and survive?

A. Leonardo da Vinci came up with the idea in 1483. However, no one succeeded in parachuting from a great height until André-Jacques Garnerin. In 1797, he proved his parachute's worth by jumping from a hot-air balloon 3,000 feet up—and making it safely to the ground.

Q. Who is considered the father of modern chemistry?

A. Antoine-Laurent Lavoisier (1743–1794). Among his many contributions was his explanation of combustion—the chemical process that creates fire—and oxygen's role in it. He also was the first to explain how animals and plants use oxygen, and why they need it to survive.

Where in the World?

UNDERGROUND

The world's first subway (a railway system built under city streets) was built in London, England. It opened on January 10, 1863.

The geographic center of the 48 contiguous U.S. states is in Smith County, Kansas. The geographic center of the 50 states is in Butte County, South Dakota.

Europe and Asia lie on the same landmass, sometimes called Eurasia. The Ural Mountains form the dividing line between the two continents.

ALASKA

Attu
ALEUTIAN
ISLANDS

The westernmost point of the U.S. is in Alaska—at Cape Wrangell, on Attu Island (one of the Aleutian Islands).

LONG ISLAND

Long Island, New York, is the largest island in the continental U.S.

Antarctica is international territory. In 1959, 12 countries signed the Antarctic Treaty, agreeing to keep Antarctica a nonmilitary zone, preserved for scientific research. Researchers work there for several months at a time, but no one lives there permanently.

The world's first boardwalk, which opened in 1870, was built in Atlantic City, New Jersey.

Four state capitals were named after U.S. presidents: Jackson, Mississippi (after Andrew Jackson); Jefferson City, Missouri (after Thomas Jefferson); Lincoln, Nebraska (after Abraham Lincoln); and Madison, Wisconsin (after James Madison).

WAY BACK WHEN

The Rosetta Stone is a stone slab that was found in Egypt in 1799. Carved into the slab was a single text in three languages—hieroglyphs, demotic (everyday Egyptian), and Greek. This helped experts figure out how to "read" ancient Egyptian hieroglyphs.

The people of ancient Egypt took 70 days to prepare a body for mummification.

On March 24, 1989, an oil tanker called the *Exxon Valdez* ran aground on a reef off the coast of Alaska. Oil that spilled from the tanker polluted 1,300 miles of shoreline.

Russians celebrate their 1917 October Revolution in November.

The first parking meter was installed in 1935 in Oklahoma City, Oklahoma.

The Renaissance was a time of greatly expanding knowledge in science and the arts. It began in Italy in the 14th century, and spread throughout Europe. The word *renaissance* (*REH-nuh-zahnts*) means "rebirth."

In 1857, New Orleans held its first Mardi Gras celebration. It started as a parade organized by a group called Mystick Krewe of Comus.

The tradition of sending written Valentine's Day messages began in the 16th century.

223

Famous Folks

Boxer Muhammad Ali's original name was Cassius Marcellus Clay Jr.

Sharpshooter Annie Oakley offered to teach marksmanship to the troops during World War I, but the government didn't take her up on the offer.

The term *sideburns* was inspired by the whiskers of a Civil War general named Ambrose Everett Burnside. Before Burnside, they were known as "side whiskers."

William Phelps Eno, known as the "Father of Traffic Safety" for creating the world's first city traffic codes, never drove a car.

Charles, the Prince of Wales, plays the cello.

The real name of the pirate known as Blackbeard was Edward Teach.

In 1778, Daniel Boone was captured by the Shawnee. His bravery impressed Chief Blackfish, who adopted him into the tribe and gave him the name *Shel-tow-ee*, which meant "Big Turtle."

The Flintstones, the Jetsons, Yogi Bear, Huckleberry Hound, and many other characters were the creations of cartoonist Joseph Barbera and writer William Hanna.

ANIMAL ANTICS

A cougar can spring 18 feet into the air—straight up!

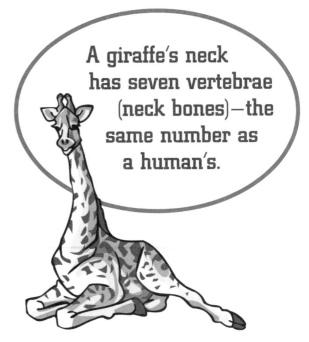

A giraffe's neck has seven vertebrae (neck bones)—the same number as a human's.

The primate most closely related to humans is the chimpanzee.

President Martin Van Buren (in office 1837–1841) once received tiger cubs as a gift.

Each dragonfly eye has up to 30,000 lenses. Each human eye has only one.

The dinosaur with the longest neck was the *Mamenchisaurus*. Its neck was about 35 feet long, roughly half its total body length.

There are no penguins in the Arctic. Wild penguins live only in the Southern Hemisphere, from Antarctica to the equator.

A pelican's pouch can hold about 12 quarts of water.

Gelada, macaque, and proboscis are three different kinds of monkey.

The grooves on the edge of the quarter are called *reeding* or *reeded edges*. The penny and the nickel are the only U.S. coins without reeding.

The world's tallest monument is the Gateway Arch in St Louis, Missouri. Built in 1965, it is 630 feet tall. It was built to honor St. Louis's historic role as "Gateway to the West."

The Easter Parade, held in New York City every Easter, is not a regular parade. It is an annual event where people gather to show off unusual spring hats.

In the ancient Japanese tradition of *ohaguro*, women blackened their teeth to be considered more beautiful.

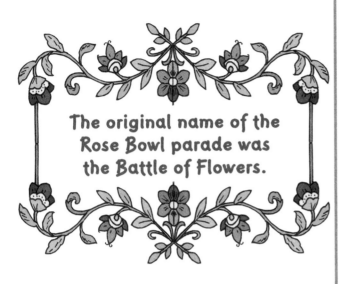

The original name of the Rose Bowl parade was the Battle of Flowers.

King Louis XIV of France, who was very short, started the fashion of wearing high-heeled shoes. (Tall wigs also were fashionable then.) High heels later faded as a style for men.

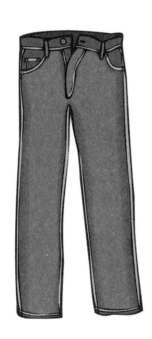

In 1850, an immigrant from Bavaria (now part of Germany) went to San Francisco to make tents for Gold Rush miners. Noticing how quickly the miners wore out their pants, he had a tailor make tougher ones out of tent canvas. Levi Strauss had created the first jeans. In 1853, he and his brothers founded the Levi Strauss & Co. Today, it is the world's largest manufacturer of pants.

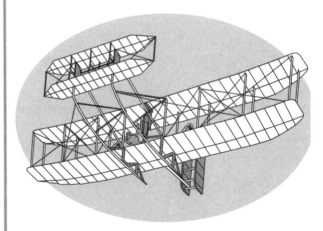

The first airplane flown by the Wright brothers at Kitty Hawk is called the Wright flyer. It can be seen at the National Air and Space Museum in Washington, D.C.

SPORTS STUFF

Q. What popular game was originally called mintonette?

A. volleyball

Q. A tennis player scoring for the first time in a match earns how many points?

A. 15

Q. How many leather panels are on a regulation soccer ball?

A. 32

Q. In 1890, boxers Danny Needham and Patsy Kerrigan fought for 6 hours and 39 minutes, until the fight was stopped and declared a draw. How many rounds was the match?

A. 100 rounds

Q. *Hang ten* is an expression used in which sport?

A. surfing (from hanging 10 toes off the edge of a surfboard)

Q. In July 1947, Larry Doby became the first African-American player in baseball's American League when he joined what team?

A. the Cleveland Indians

Q. How many batters does a pitcher face in a perfect game?— no runs, no hits, no errors, no walks, and no batters hit.

A. 27

Q. Where were the first outdoor miniature-golf courses built?

A. on New York City rooftops, in 1926

Q. When an ice-hockey player scores three goals in one game, what is it called?

A. a hat trick

231

ANYONE HUNGRY?

Chinese gooseberry is another name for the kiwi fruit.

Brazil grows the most bananas—about ten million tons per year.

Wisconsin produces about two billion pounds of cheese each year.

In Japan, eel and squid are popular pizza toppings.

Akutaq (pronounced *ah-goo-dik*) is also known as Eskimo ice cream. This tribal Alaskan treat is not made with cream, however. Its ingredients include dried caribou, moose, or reindeer fat; seal, walrus, or whale oil; and berries. Some recipes include salmon eggs, fish liver, or greens.

Americans eat about 1.2 billion pounds of potato chips—their favorite snack food—each year.

Wild rice is not really rice. It is a coarse grass found in shallow, marshy lakes and streams.

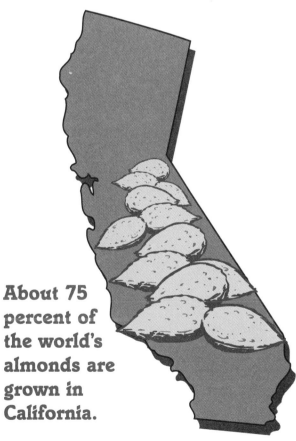

Have you ever heard the saying, "cool as a cucumber"? That is pretty cool, indeed. The temperature inside a cucumber can be 20 degrees cooler than the outside air!

About 75 percent of the world's almonds are grown in California.

TV, Movies, Music, & More

William Shakespeare never saw an actress perform in any of his plays. During his time, all roles were performed by males.

Now a movie star, Leonardo DiCaprio made his TV debut at age five on *Romper Room,* a popular children's television show.

Bruce Lee, a martial-arts film star, was so fast, filmmakers slowed the film so viewers could see his moves.

The first screening of a giant-screen IMAX movie was in 1970 at the Fuji Pavilion in Osaka, Japan. The screening took place during Expo '70, Japan's first world's fair.

The American play and movie *West Side Story* was based on William Shakespeare's play *Romeo and Juliet*.

Sleeping Beauty's real name was Princess Aurora.

The first thing that Winnie-the-Pooh says to himself when he wakes up each morning is, "What's for breakfast?"

On January 7, 1955, Marian Anderson became the first African-American singer to perform as a member of the Metropolitan Opera in New York City.

"Twinkle, Twinkle, Little Star," a children's song still popular today, was composed by Wolfgang Amadeus Mozart when he was five years old.

ANIMAL ANTICS

The vampire bat, which lives in Central and South America and survives on blood, can drink its own weight in blood. A two-ounce vampire bat can weigh four ounces after just one feeding!

The name *millipede* means "thousand feet." In reality, however, a millipede has, at most, 400 legs—and as few as 8.

Ostriches lay eggs that average 3 pounds each. A full-grown ostrich can be 8 feet tall and weigh up to 300 pounds, making it the world's largest living bird.

President Thomas Jefferson kept grizzly bears on the White House grounds—but not for long. He had to give them away when winter came. The two cubs had been a gift from explorer Zebulon Pike.

236

A giraffe cleans its own ears—with its 18-inch-long tongue!

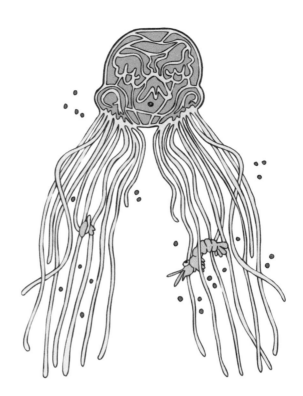

Jellyfish are 95 percent water. They have no bones, no heart, no brain, and no eyes.

Male and female pigeons share the job of incubating their eggs. Often, they take turns sitting on the eggs. Sometimes, they do it together. When the eggs hatch, both parents feed the young.

A slug has four noses.

Some kinds of starfish turn their stomachs inside out to eat.

WHAT'S THE WORD?

Triskaidekaphobia (tris-kye-dek-uh-FOH-bee-uh) is an exaggerated or illogical fear of the number 13.

The English word *honcho* comes from the Japanese word *hancho*, which means "squad leader."

OH NO, I'M LOSING MY SALT!

The word *khaki*, used to describe a light-brown fabric, originated in India. (It is a Hindi word meaning "dust-colored.")

The English word *salary* comes from *salarium*, a Latin word meaning "salt allowance." Salt was a valued part of a Roman soldier's rations.

Shakespeare was the first writer known to use many now-common words, including *alligator*, *lonely*, and *watchdog*.

The word in the English language with the most definitions is *set*. The *Oxford English Dictionary* has 464 definitions for it!

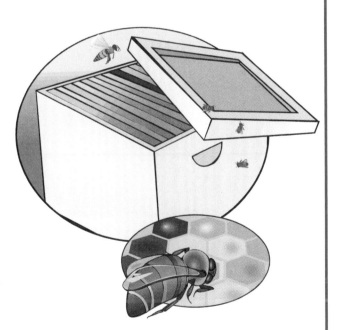

An *apiary* is not a monkey house—it is a home for bees. The name comes from *apis*, the Latin word for "bee."

Strike the sails is a sailors' term meaning "lower the sails." Doing so makes a wind-driven ship unable to move. In 1768, protesting seamen struck their sails to show their refusal to go to sea. That gave the word *strike* a new meaning: to stop working as a form of protest.

Nature Notes

Q. How deep is the ocean?

A. 36,201 feet (at Earth's lowest point, the Mariana Trench in the western North Pacific Ocean)

Q. How many sides (or branches) does a snowflake have?

A. six

Q. Is there such a thing as red rain?

A. Yes. Winds blow red dust from the Sahara Desert high into the air. Water vapor condenses around the dust and falls, in parts of Europe, as red rain.

Q. How long does it take to boil a three-minute egg in Denver, Colorado?

A. four minutes (The higher the altitude, the lower the air pressure—and the longer it takes water to boil.)

Q. Which planet in our solar system spins backward?

A. Venus (Viewed from above its north pole, Venus spins clockwise. The other planets spin counterclockwise.)

Q. The state with the record maximum precipitation in a year is Hawaii. Which state has the record minimum annual precipitation?

A. California (California had 0.00 inches in 1929. Hawaii had 704.83 inches in 1982.)

Q. How many thunderstorms, on average, are crackling and zapping around the world at any given moment?

A. 2,000

Q. Which area is home to more penguins, the North Pole or the South Pole?

A. the South Pole (All penguins live in the Southern Hemisphere. There are none at the North Pole.)

241

The Amazing U.S.A.

Eleven slave states seceded from the Union and joined the Confederate States of America in 1860–1861.

Francis Scott Key is famous for writing the words to "The Star-Spangled Banner," but he was not a songwriter or poet. He was a lawyer by profession.

The U.S. Weather Bureau was established in 1891. It was an off-shoot of the first national weather service, created in 1870 by the U.S. Army Signal Service.

The U.S. Coast Guard Academy was the first U.S. military service academy to admit women (in 1976).

The animal symbols of the two main U.S. political parties—a donkey for the Democratic Party and an elephant for the Republican Party—were created by Thomas Nast (1840–1902).

The U.S. consumes about 25 percent of the world's energy. It has about 5 percent of the world's population.

About 200,000 African-Americans served in the Union Army during the Civil War.

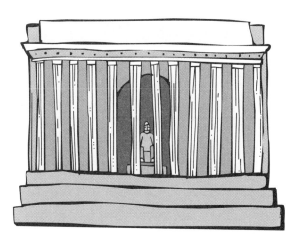

The image of the Lincoln Memorial was put on the back of the U.S. penny in 1959—50 years after Abraham Lincoln's image was put on the front side.

It took the *Mayflower* 66 days to sail from England to America in 1620.

ANIMAL ANTICS

A newborn kangaroo is only one inch long.

No two zebras have stripes that are exactly alike. A zebra's stripe pattern is like a human's fingerprints; no two are the same.

The mosquito is responsible for more human deaths, worldwide, than any other animal—mostly by spreading malaria.

The smallest type of whale, the dwarf sperm whale, is about 8.5 feet long.

In a wolf pack, *alpha* refers to the most forceful, powerful male and/or female that rules the pack and makes decisions necessary for the pack's survival.

About 20 million Mexican free-tailed bats roost in Texas's Bracken Cave.

Each day, about 800 dolphins, porpoises, and whales get caught in fishing nets and drown.

The zoo with the largest collection of animals in North America is in San Diego, California.

The little brown bat, which weighs less than one-fifth of an ounce, can eat about 600 mosquito-sized insects in just one hour.

245

TV, Movies, Music, & More

Q. What are Batman's and Robin's real names?

A. Bruce Wayne (Batman) and Dick Grayson (Robin)

Q. Who was left in charge when the Wizard of Oz left the Emerald City?

A. the Scarecrow

Q. What is the name of Spiderman's true identity?

A. Peter Parker

Q. Where were the baby Harry Potter and his parents when they were attacked by Lord Voldemort?

A. Godric's Hollow

Q. Popeye the Sailor gets his super strength from eating spinach. What food gave his ancestor, Popeye Hercules, super strength?

A. garlic (He sniffed it.)

Q. What happened to the Three Blind Mice of nursery-rhyme fame?

A. Their tails were cut off by the farmer's wife.

Q. Ian Fleming, an author who was a British spy during World War II, created what famous fictional spy?

A. James Bond, agent 007

Q. The Beatles starred as cartoon characters in what full-length animated film?

A. *Yellow Submarine* (first released in 1968)

Q. In the Grimm brothers' fairy tale "Hansel and Gretel," who pushed the witch into the oven?

A. Gretel

247

Science Fair

An *otolaryngologist (OH-toh-lar-un-GAH-luh-jist)* is a medical doctor who specializes in treatment of the ear, nose, and throat.

In 1642, Blaise Pascal, a French mathematician and scientist, invented the first mechanical calculator. His invention is called a "digital arithmetic machine."

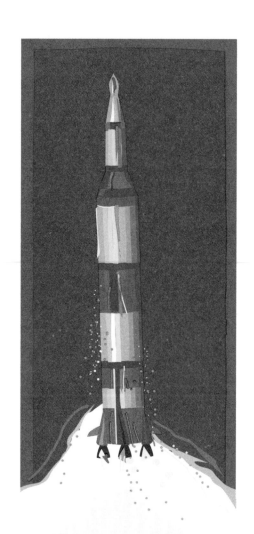

A space vehicle must move at least seven miles per second to escape Earth's gravity. This is called *escape velocity.*

The closest galaxy to Earth's own Milky Way is the Andromeda Galaxy, which is about 2,000,000 light-years away. It is one of the few galaxies that can be seen from Earth with the naked eye.

Banana oil is not made from bananas. Its name comes from the fact that it smells like bananas.

William Stewart Halsted, the developer of local anesthesia, was the first doctor to use thin rubber gloves during surgery (in 1890). Halsted also founded the first surgical school in the U.S.

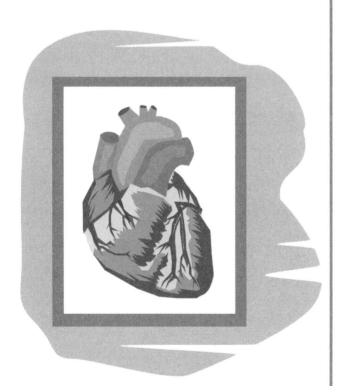

In 1893, Dr. Daniel Hale Williams performed the first successful operation on a human heart.

A nautical (at-sea) mile is 6,076 feet long. (A regular mile is 5,280 feet.)

WAY BACK WHEN

People of ancient Egypt believed that mothers were the gods' gift to Earth.

The first printed Christmas card was sent by Sir Henry Cole in 1843. John Calcott Horsley designed it according to Sir Henry's request.

Only two parts of North America were occupied by Japanese troops during World War II: Attu and Kiska, two of the Aleutian Islands off the coast of Alaska.

Pan American was the first airline to serve hot meals during a flight.

The Eiffel Tower was built in 1887–1889. Nearly 1,000 feet tall, it was the world's tallest structure until 1930.

In 1698, Peter the Great, leader of Russia, wanted men to shave, so he imposed a tax on beards. The tax applied to all men except priests and peasants.

Paper currency (money) was first used in China, about A.D. 806.

In 1964, Baskin-Robbins created a special ice-cream flavor to celebrate the Beatles' arrival in the U.S. It was called Beatle Nut—after *betel nut*, a seed whose name is pronounced the same way as the band's.

SPORTS STUFF

An official soccer ball weighs 14 to 16 ounces.

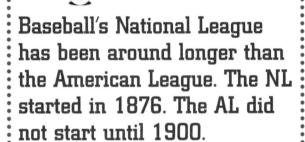

Baseball's National League has been around longer than the American League. The NL started in 1876. The AL did not start until 1900.

Babe Ruth trained to work as a tailor—in case he didn't succeed in baseball.

Miniature golf was originally called "Rinkiedink" golf. (The first chain of miniature-golf courses was called Tom Thumb Golf.)

Since 1936, a bottle of milk has been the traditional drink served in the winner's circle at the Indianapolis 500.

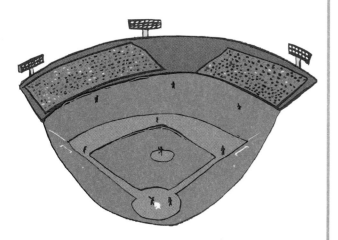

The shortest nine-inning game in major-league base-ball lasted only 1 hour, 53 minutes. It took place on July 9, 1940, at Sportsman's Park in St. Louis, Missouri.

The first five players to be inducted into base-ball's National Hall of Fame were Ty Cobb, Walter Johnson, Christy Mathewson, Babe Ruth, and Honus Wagner, all in 1936.

Baseball and tennis are two sports that are *not* played against the clock.

The most lopsided score in a college football game was 222–0. Georgia Tech's thrashing of Cumberland University took place on October 7, 1916, in Atlanta, Georgia.

ANIMAL ANTICS

Q. What sea creature rarely gets sick and seems to be immune to all known diseases?

A. the shark

Q. What type of whale has a spiraled tusk (up to 10 feet long) like a unicorn's?

A. the male narwhal

Q. Do polar bears hibernate in winter?

A. no

Q. How many arms does an octopus have?

A. eight

Q. What type of insect can live the longest?

A. the king and queen termite, which can live 60 to 70 years

Q. Does a painted turtle swallow its food above or below water?

A. below water (the same as other species of turtle)

Q. Which U.S. state raises the most turkeys?

A. Minnesota

Q. What kind of sound does a giraffe make?

A. a low moan

Q. What color attracts mosquitoes?

A. blue

Nature Notes

A fluid that that looks, feels, and tastes like milk can be found in the *Brosimum utile*, a tree that grows in the tropics of Central and South America. No wonder it also is known as the cow tree or as *palo de vaca*, which means "cow stick"!

The tallest living trees in the world are redwoods that grow along the Pacific coast, from southwestern Oregon to central California. Some are taller than 300 feet! Supporting all that height are trunks that can be 20 or more feet across.

If you could see a rainbow from above, it would be shaped like a doughnut.

The potato is related to the petunia.

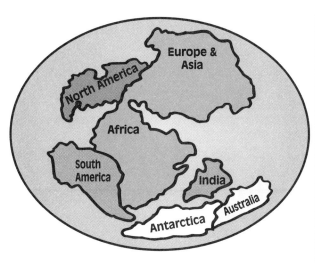

About 300 million years ago, all the land on Earth was probably a single landmass surrounded by a vast ocean. Over time that landmass, known as Pangaea *(pan-JEE-uh)*, broke apart. The pieces drifted apart, forming the continents as we know them today.

Earth's atmosphere has five levels: the **troposphere** (0–7 miles high), the **stratosphere** (7–30 miles high), the **mesosphere** (30–50 miles high), the **thermosphere** (50–120 miles high), and the **exosphere** (120–600 miles high).

If you count the seconds between a flash of lightning and the thunder that follows, then divide that number by five, you will know about how many miles away the lightning struck.

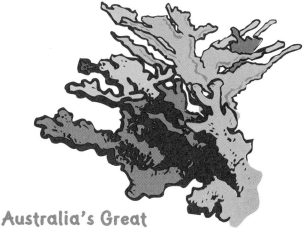

Australia's Great Barrier Reef is the largest structure in the world built by living creatures. The reef, which is 1,250 miles long, was created by polyps. These tiny sea animals form skeletons, called corals, around their bodies. When they die, the corals grow together, forming a reef.

Science Fair

In 1781, William Herschel discovered the planet Uranus—the first new planet to be discovered since prehistoric times. In 1800, Herschel announced another important discovery: infrared light.

The next time your mother puts antiseptic on a cut or sore, don't think about the sting—thank Dr. Joseph Lister instead. In 1867, he introduced the practice of using antiseptics during surgery. Before then, countless people died of infections that set in after surgery.

258

The sun is so hot that anything solid or liquid would be burned up instantly. That fiery ball of gas is huge. Its radius (the distance from center to surface) is about 432,500 miles.

Industrial robotics began in 1954, when George C. Devol designed the first programmable robot. In 1962, General Motors became the first corporation to buy an industrial robot—for use on its production line.

Have you ever seen "gaffer" and "best boy" in a movie's credits, and wondered what they do? The gaffer is an electrician who is responsible for the lighting used on a film or TV set. The best boy (male or female) is the gaffer's chief assistant.

In 1945, while working in a lab, Percy Spencer stood in front of a magnetron (a device used to generate power). The chocolate bar in his pocket melted—even though he felt no heat. Spencer realized that microwaves from the magnetron had done it, and an invention was born.

The human nose can recognize about 10,000 different smells.

The human body has about 5.2 million red blood cells per cubic millimeter of blood. How small is that? One millimeter is about one twenty-fifth of an inch!

How tough are your teeth? They are almost as hard as rock. Their outer layer, called enamel, is the hardest tissue in the body.

If the average man never shaved or trimmed his beard, it would grow about 30 feet in his lifetime.

The sound that you hear when holding a seashell to your ear is the echo of your blood pulsing in your ear.

In scientific terms, the word *pulmonary* refers to the lungs.

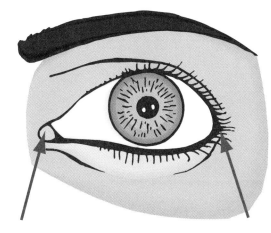

Each corner of the human eye, where the upper and lower lids meet, is called a *canthus*.

If three inches of hair was cut off during your last haircut, it will take about six months to grow back. Human hair grows at a rate of about six inches a year.

DNA (deoxyribonucleic acid) is the substance that tells a body's cells how to behave.

The Amazing U.S.A.

Oregon grows more Christmas trees than any other U.S. state—nearly nine million a year.

The first U.S. census was taken in 1790. It showed a population of 3,929,214 people.

It's official: Americans love apples! In New York, Rhode Island, Vermont, Washington, and West Virginia, the apple is the official state fruit. The apple blossom is the state flower in Arkansas and Michigan. New York's state muffin is the apple muffin, and Vermont's state pie what else?—the apple pie.

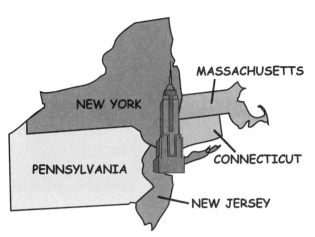

On a clear day, parts of five states can be seen from the top of the Empire State Building in New York City: New York, New Jersey, Pennsylvania, Connecticut, and Massachusetts.

Louisiana is the only U.S. state to have parishes instead of counties.

The Statue of Liberty stands 152 feet tall (305 feet, counting the pedestal)—and her nose is 4.5 feet long.

Each Thanksgiving, Americans eat more pumpkin pie than any other kind of pie.

Benjamin and *C-note* are two slang words for a $100 bill. *Benjamin* is for Benjamin Franklin, whose face is on the bill. *C* is the Roman numeral for 100.

The Dutch and Swedes were the first Europeans to settle in New Jersey.

THIS and THAT

The F-117A Nighthawk, a stealth fighter, has no guns. (It does have a variety of other weaponry, including laser-guided bombs.)

Henry I, king of England from 1100 to 1135, declared that a foot would be equal to one-third the length of his arm. This set a standard for a unit of measurement that had varied till then.

The Ford Motor Company once raised sheep—to provide wool for its cars' upholstery.

According to the Old Testament of the Bible, Moses was 120 years old when he died.

A baby's cry can be up to 110 decibels loud—the same level as a power saw. That is louder than an electric drill (95 decibels), a hair dryer (60-95 decibels), and even a tractor (90 decibels)!

The image of Santa Claus as we recognize him today was created by cartoonist Thomas Nast, who lived 1840–1902.

At 16,730 feet above sea level, Wenzhuan, China, is the highest town in the world.

New York's Empire State Building has 73 elevators—including 6 freight elevators.

The famous winged horse of Greek mythology is named Pegasus.

PRESIDENTS ON PARADE

The longest presidential convention was the Democratic Party's 1924 convention. It lasted 17 days and took 103 ballots (rounds of voting) before the conventioneers chose a candidate, John Davis. Davis lost the national election to Republican Calvin Coolidge.

Jimmy Carter was the first president to report a UFO sighting. Carter, who was elected president in 1976, filed an official sighting report in 1973, while he was the governor of Georgia.

In 1880, Rutherford B. Hayes became the first U.S. president to use a presidential seal. In 1945, Harry S. Truman (above) was the first president to use the seal with the current design.

Our American Cousin is the name of the play that President Abraham Lincoln was watching when he was shot on April 14, 1865. He died the next morning.

Mount Vernon is the home and burial place of the first U.S. president. George Washington's family estate in Fairfax County, Virginia, is now a national registered historic landmark.

At 6'4", Abraham Lincoln was the tallest U.S. president. At 5'4", James Madison was the shortest.

George Washington's salary as president was $25,000 per year.

In 1931, President Herbert Hoover signed a bill making "The Star-Spangled Banner" the national anthem of the United States.

John Tyler fathered 15 children—more than any other U.S. president. (He had eight with his first wife, Letitia Gardiner Tyler, and seven with his second wife, Julia Gardiner Tyler.)

ANYONE HUNGRY?

Q. Which vegetable, once called the "mad apple," was long thought to be poisonous?

A. the eggplant

Q. What gives a bagel a shiny crust?

A. Before the ring-shaped dough is baked, it is boiled or steamed, then glazed with egg yolk or milk.

Q. What does the Food and Drug Administration (FDA) require commercial ice cream to contain in order to be called ice cream?

A. at least 10 percent butterfat

Q. The flesh of what vegetable may be purple, yellow, or white?

A. the potato

Q. How much candy do Americans eat in a year?

A. about 7 billion pounds—an average of 24 pounds for every man, woman, and child in the U.S.

Q. What is a love apple?

A. the 19th-century name for a tomato

Q. How can you tell a hard-boiled egg from an uncooked one?

A. Put them side by side and spin them. The one that spins longest is hard-boiled. (The liquid inside the raw egg sloshes around inside, slowing it down.)

Q. A peanut is not really a nut. What is it?

A. It is a legume (as are peas and beans). A legume is the pod fruit of certain plants, while a nut is a hard dry fruit with a single seed inside.

Q. Which of the following is not a fruit: cucumbers, pumpkins, rhubarb, or tomatoes?

A. rhubarb (It is an edible leafstalk.)

ANIMAL ANTICS

A silkworm is not a worm. It is a caterpillar, which later becomes a moth.

The 150-pound Pacific giant octopus can squeeze its entire body through an opening no bigger than the width of its eye.

The smallest living bird is the bee hummingbird—only about two inches long. It weighs only seven hundredths (0.07) of an ounce!

The basilisk, a type of lizard, can run on the surface of water.

An adult male bear is called a boar. An adult female bear is called a sow.

Antelopes, cows, giraffes, deer, and sheep are all ruminants—cud-chewing animals with four-chambered stomachs and two-toed feet.

Baby sharks are called pups.

Honeybees must make about 35,000 trips from flower to hive in order to produce one pound of honey.

Some scientists think that *Tyrannosaurus rex* could rip off a 500-pound chunk of meat with just one bite of its powerful jaws.

Nature Notes

Natural gas has no odor. An odor is artificially added so that we can smell any leaks.

The sun provides more than enough energy in one minute to supply enough for the entire world's use for a year.

The weightlessness of space makes an astronaut taller! Without the pressure of gravity, the spine straightens, making a person taller. Once back on Earth, however, the astronaut goes back to normal size.

Kelp (a type of seaweed) may be the fastest-growing plant on Earth. It can grow up to 18 inches in a single day!

Each minute, about 40 million gallons of water spill over Niagara Falls.

A man is four times as likely to be struck by lightning than a woman is.

Twenty-five percent of all the world's forests can be found in Siberia.

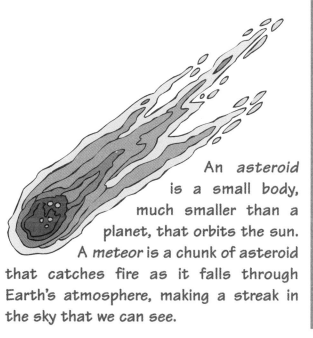

An *asteroid* is a small body, much smaller than a planet, that orbits the sun. A *meteor* is a chunk of asteroid that catches fire as it falls through Earth's atmosphere, making a streak in the sky that we can see.

The banana plant is an herb, not a tree. (Trees have woody stems; herbs do not.) In fact, banana plants are the biggest herbs on Earth—their trunklike stems can grow 10 to 20 feet high.

Famous Folks

The first woman to win a Nobel Peace Prize was Baroness Bertha Felicie Sophie von Suttner, in 1905. She belonged to or helped found a number of peace organizations, wrote many books and articles opposing war, and traveled the world calling on people to unite rather than fight.

Though famous for her humanitarian work in India, Mother Teresa was born and raised in Albania. (Her original name was Agnes Gonxha Bojaxhiu.)

Liliuokalani *(lih-LEE-uh-woh-kuh-LAH-nee)* was the first and last queen to rule Hawaii. Heir to a long line of Hawaiian kings, she took the throne in 1877 and ruled until the U.S. took control of Hawaii in 1898. She wrote "Aloha Oe," the most famous Hawaiian song.

In 138 B.C.—long before Marco Polo—Zhang Qian set off on a mission for China's emperor. He traveled thousands of miles, returning home 13 years later. Zhang's knowledge of faraway lands and peoples helped open a major trade route between China and Rome: the Silk Road. It was an important Asia–Europe link for many centuries.

The first female chief of a large Native American tribe was Wilma Mankiller. She became principal chief of the Cherokee Nation in 1985, and served in that post until 1995. She was inducted into the National Women's Hall of Fame in 1993.

Now worth more than 45 billion dollars, Bill Gates has been the world's wealthiest person for most of the last two decades. The bulk of his fortune comes from Microsoft Corporation, the huge computer-software company that he cofounded in the 1970s.

The first successful hot-air balloon was built by two brothers, Joseph-Michel and Jacques-Étienne Montgolfier. The first manned flight of a Montgolfier-built balloon took place on November 21, 1783.

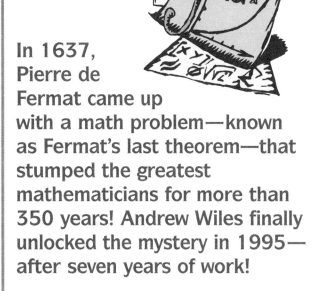

In 1637, Pierre de Fermat came up with a math problem—known as Fermat's last theorem—that stumped the greatest mathematicians for more than 350 years! Andrew Wiles finally unlocked the mystery in 1995—after seven years of work!

WAY BACK WHEN

Q. When did Rome become the capital of Italy?

A. in 1870

Q. What product did Napoleon have developed for his army, navy, and the needy people of France?

A. margarine (In 1869, a chemist named Hippolyte Mège-Mouriès won the prize offered by Napoleon for inventing a butter substitute.)

Q. Who was the French citizen, closely associated with George Washington, who fought with the Continental Army during the American Revolution?

A. the Marquis de Lafayette (His full name was Marie-Joseph-Paul-Yves-Roch-Gilbert du Motier. His title was the Marquis of Lafayette.)

Q. What famous explorer sailed in a ship called the *Half Moon*?

A. Henry Hudson

Q. The wheelbarrow probably was invented where?

A. in ancient China (No one knows for sure, but its invention has been credited to Chuko Liang, who lived in A.D. 181-234.)

Q. How did the name "John Hancock" become a slang term for a signature?

A. Hancock was the first person to sign the Declaration of Independence in 1776. His signature appears first on the page, and is the largest.

Q. In ancient Egypt, how did a family mourn when a pet cat died?

A. They shaved their eyebrows.

Q. What 3,000-mile trip did George Samuelson and Frank Harbo complete in a rowboat in 1896?

A. They rowed from New York to England (in 56 days).

Q. How many vessels sailed with Christopher Columbus on his second voyage to the New World?

A. 17

SPORTS STUFF

The largest football stadium of any U.S. university belongs to the University of Michigan. Michigan Stadium has a capacity of 102,501 people.

All members of a baseball team can have the identical batting average before and after a game! That would be the case if the game were the first of the season and every member of the team performed the same way in every at bat. For example, if every player went 1-for-4 in the game, every player would have a .250 batting average. If a no-hitter was pitched against that team, every player would have a batting average of zero—same as before the game.

In golf, the official size of a hole is 4.25 inches across and at least 4 inches deep.

The only basketball star to play his entire 14-season NBA career—postseason as well as regular-season games—without fouling out was Wilt Chamberlain.

Curling became a full medal Olympic sport at the 1998 Games in Nagano, Japan. What is curling? It's something like bowling on ice, using objects called stones instead of bowling balls. Teammates with brooms try to help the stone along without touching it. The team that gets its stones closest to the center ring wins the game.

The first Rose Bowl game took place in 1902.

Night baseball games began in 1935, at Crosley Field in Cincinnati.

The maximum allowable length of a major-league bat is 42 inches.

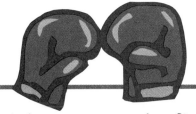

Jack Johnson was the first African-American heavyweight boxing champion. He won the title on December 26, 1908.

The Amazing U.S.A.

U.S. paper money is composed
of 25 percent linen and
75 percent cotton.

Wyoming was the first state to
allow women to vote. That was in
1869. The right of U.S. women to
vote was not granted nationwide
until 1920.

Settlers from Sweden taught
Native Americans how to build
log cabins, about 1638.

The highest award that
a U.S. soldier can receive is
the Medal of Honor.

The first roller coaster in the U.S. was built in 1884, in Brooklyn, New York.

Ninety-five percent of Americans have turkey for Thanksgiving dinner.

On July 4, 1776, John Dunlap printed the first official copies of the Declaration of Independence. Twenty-four of Dunlap's originals, known as the Dunlap Broadsides, are known to exist today. Two are in the Library of Congress.

Americans throw away plastic bottles at a rate of 2.5 million an hour.

SPEND ME WHILE YOU CAN. I RETIRE IN 18 MONTHS!

The average life of a one-dollar bill is 18 months.

Where in the World?

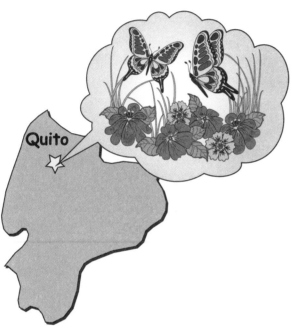

Quito

The city of Quito, Ecuador, is known as the Land of Eternal Spring, because its climate is pleasant all year-round.

Lombard Street of San Francisco, California, is considered to be the most crooked street in the world. It has its eight consecutive 90-degree turns.

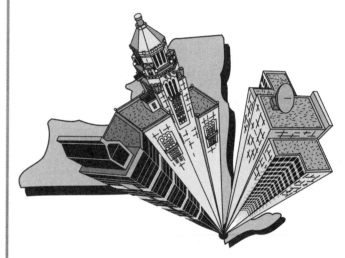

New York City holds the world record for the most skyscrapers.

From shore to shore, the Panama Canal is 40 miles long.

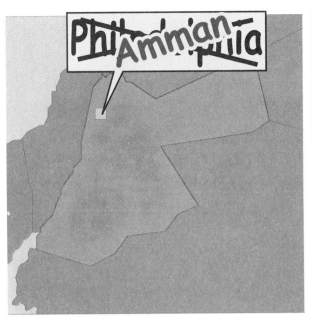

Amman, the capital of Jordan, was once called Philadelphia.

The most densely populated state in the U.S. is New Jersey, with 1,134.4 people per square mile (according to the 2000 Census).

The world's longest continuous border—4,254 miles long—is between Russia and Kazakhstan.

The city that was Egypt's capital from about 2575 to 2130 B.C. and a city in Tennessee have the same name: Memphis. The Tennessee city was named for the Egyptian one, because both sit on mighty rivers. Memphis, Tennessee, was built on the Mississippi; Memphis, Egypt, was built on the Nile.

The world's longest road tunnel is the St. Gotthard Tunnel, in the Alps. It is 10.2 miles long.

The Amazing U.S.A.

Capitol Building

The 19.5-foot-tall statue on top of the U.S. Capitol building is named *Freedom*.

Morocco was the first country to recognize the United States as a sovereign nation. It did so in 1777, soon after the American colonies declared their independence.

The first American newspaper was *Publick Occurrences*, published in Boston, Massachusetts, in 1690. Only one issue was published.

To get from France, where it was built, to the U.S., the 152-foot, 225-ton Statue of Liberty had to be broken down into 350 pieces. Packed into 214 crates, it sailed for New York in 1885.

NEW YORK

The top of the Empire State Building was originally designed to hold a mooring for blimps. Windy conditions forced planners to abandon the idea.

Boston Common, in Boston, Massachusetts, is the oldest public park in the U.S.

The U.S. produces more than 790 million pounds of pumpkin a year. The state that produces the largest number of pumpkins is Illinois.

Frances Perkins was the first woman appointed to a U.S. Cabinet post. She served as the U.S. Secretary of Labor from 1933 to 1945.

ANIMAL ANTICS

Q. A male swan is called a cob. A female swan is called a pen. What is a baby swan called?

A. a cygnet (SIG-nut)

Q. Does a mosquito have teeth?

A. No, but a mosquito's mouthparts do have sharp, jagged edges that help it pierce the skin.

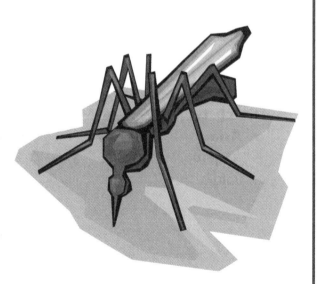

Q. What type of dog, known to us today, existed in ancient Egypt?

A. the greyhound (A picture of one, on a tomb, dates from about 3000 B.C.)

Q. Which animal has the sharpest sense of hearing: a dog, a dolphin, or a rabbit?

A. a dolphin. Its auditory (hearing) nerve can have 67,900 or more cochlear fibers—twice as many as in the human auditory nerve.

Q. Each elephant has something that is different from every other elephant's—as different as fingerprints are in humans. What is it?

A. the elephant's ears

Q. Do all snakes lay eggs?

A. No. Some snake species, such as the garter snake, give birth to live babies.

Q. What bird is the mascot of the U.S. Air Force Academy?

A. the falcon

Q. Which type of elephant, African or Asian, has the larger ears?

A. the African elephant, which is the largest living land animal

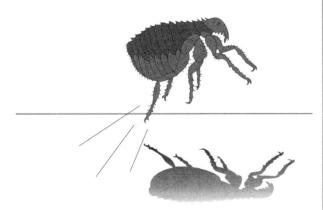

Q. How far can a flea fly?

A. The flea is a wingless insect. It can't fly, it can only jump.

287